The Old Bachelor by William Congreve

A COMEDY

William Congreve was born on January 24th, 1670 in Bardsey, West Yorkshire.

Congreve's childhood was spent in Ireland (his father, a Lieutenant in the British Army had received a posting there). He was educated at Kilkenny College and then Trinity College in Dublin.

After graduating he returned to London to study law at Middle Temple. However his interest in studying law soon lessened as the attraction of literature, drama, and the fashionable life began to exert its pull.

This first play, The Old Bachelor, was written, to amuse himself during convalescence, and was produced at the Drury Lane Theatre in 1693. It was an enormous success.

Although his playwrighting career was successful it was also very brief. Five plays authored from 1693 to 1700 would prove the entirety of his output.

Although no further plays were to flow from his pen Congreve did write librettos for two operas and to begin translating the works of Molière as well as Homer, Ovid and Horace and to write poetry.

He also took an interest in politics and obtained various minor political posts, including being named Secretary of the Island of Jamaica by George I in 1714.

Congreve suffered a carriage accident in late September 1728, from which he never recovered (having probably received an internal injury);

William Congreve died in London on January 19th, 1729, and was buried in Poets' Corner in Westminster Abbey.

Index of Contents

INTRODUCTION

I

Before repeating such known facts of Congreve's life as seem agreeable to the present occasion, and before attempting (with the courage of one's office) to indicate with truth what manner of man he was, and what are the varying qualities of his four comedies, it seems well to discuss and have done with two questions, obviously pertinent indeed, but of a wider scope than the works of any one writer.

The first is a stupid question, which may be happily dismissed with brief ceremony. Grossness of language—the phrase is an assumption—is a matter of time and place, a relative matter altogether. There is a thing, and a generation finds a name for it. The delicacy which prompts a later generation to reject that name is by no means necessarily a result of stricter habits, is far more often due to the flatness which comes of untiring repetition and to the greater piquancy of litotes. I am told that there are, or were, people in America who reject the word 'leg' as a gross word, but they must have found a synonym. So there is not a word in Congreve for which there is not some equivalent expression in contemporary writing. He says this or that: your modern writers say so-and-so. One man may even think the monosyllables in better taste than the periphrases. Another may sacrifice to his intolerance thereof such enjoyment as he was capable of taking from the greatest triumphs of diction or observation: he is free to choose. It may be granted that to one unfamiliar with the English of two centuries since the grossness of Congreve's language may seem excessive—like splashes of colour occurring too frequently in the arrangement of a wall. But that is merely a result of novelty: given time and habit, a more artistic perspective will be achieved.

The second question is more complex. Since Jeremy Collier let off his Short View of the Immorality and Profaneness of the English Stage, there has never lacked a critic to chastise or to deplore—the more effective and irritating course—not simply the coarseness but, the immorality of our old comedies, their attitude towards and their peculiar interests in life. Without affirming that we are now come to the Golden Age of criticism, one may rejoice that modern methods have taught quite humble critics to discriminate between issues, and to deal with such a matter as this with some mental detachment. The great primal fallacy comes from a habit of expecting everything in everything. Just as in a picture it is not enough for some people that it is well drawn and well painted, but they demand an interesting story, a fine sentiment, a great thought: so since our national glory is understood to be the happy home, the happy home must be triumphant everywhere, even in satiric comedy. The best expression of this fallacy is in Thackeray. Concluding a most eloquent, and a somewhat patronising examination of Congreve, 'Ah!' he exclaims, 'it's a weary feast, that banquet of wit where no love is.' The answer is plain: comedy of manners is comedy of manners, and satire is satire; introduce 'love'—an appeal, one supposes, to sympathy with strictly legitimate and common affection and a glorification of the happy home—and the rules of your art compel you to satirise affection and to make the happy home ridiculous: a truly deplorable work, which the incriminated dramatists were discreet enough for the most part to avoid. The remark brings us to the first of the half-truths, which cause the complexity of the subject. The dramatists whose withers the well-intentioned and disastrous Collier wrung seem to have thought their best answer was to pose as people with a mission—certainly Congreve so posed—to reform the world with an exhibition of its follies. An amusing answer, no doubt, of which the absurdity is obvious! It does, however, contain a half-truth. The idea of The Way of the World's reforming adulterers—observe the quotation from Horace on the title-page—is a little delicious; yet the exhibition in a ludicrous light of the thing satirised is surely an end of satiric comedy? The right of the matter is indicated in a sentence which occurs in the dedication of The Double-Dealer far more wisely than in Congreve's answer to Collier: 'I should be very glad of an opportunity to make my compliment to those ladies who are offended: but they can no more expect it in a comedy, than to be tickled by a surgeon, when he's letting 'em blood.' Something more than a half-truth is in Charles Lamb's theory, that the old comedy 'has no reference whatever to the world that is': that it is 'the Utopia of Gallantry' merely. Literally, historically, the theory is a fantasy. What the Restoration dramatists did not borrow from France was inspired directly by the court of Charles the Second, and nobody conversant with the memoirs of that court can have any difficulty in matching the fiction with reality. I imagine that Congreve in part accepted a tradition of the stage, but I am also perfectly well assured that he depicted what he saw. How far the virtues we should associate with the Charles the Second spirit may atone for its vices is a question which would take us far into moral philosophy. It is enough to remark that those vices are the exclusive possession of no period: so long as society is constituted in anything like its present order, there must be a section of it for which those vices are the main interest in life. But Charles Lamb's gay and engaging defiance of the kill-joys of his day has this value: it is most certainly just to say that, in appreciating satiric comedy, 'our coxcombical moral sense' must be 'for a little transitory ease excluded.'

For one may apprehend the whole truth to be somewhat thus. Satiric comedy, or comedy of manners, is the art of making ludicrous in dramatic form some phase of life. The writers of our old comedy thought that certain vices—gambling, adultery, and the like—formed a phase of life which for divers reasons, essential and accidental, lent itself best to their purpose. They may, or may not, have thought they were doing society a service: their real justification is that, as artists, they had to take for their art that material they could use best. They used it according to their lights: Wycherley with a coarse and heavy hand, so that it became nauseous; Etherege with a light touch and a gay perception; Congreve with an instinct of good-breeding, with a sure and extensive observation, and with an incomparable style. But all were justified in choosing for their material just what they chose. They sinned artistically, now here, now there; but to complain of this old comedy as a whole, that vice in it is crammed too closely, is to forget that a play is a picture, not a photograph, of life—is life arranged and coloured—and that comedy of manners is composed of foibles or vices condensed and relieved by one another. In so far as they overdid this work, the comic writers were artistically at fault, and Jeremy Collier was a good critic; but when he and his successors go beyond the artistic objection, one takes leave to say, they misapprehend the thing criticised. To complain that 'love' and common morality have no place in satiric comedy is either to contemplate ridicule of them or to ask comedy to be other than satiric. We know what happened when the dramatists gave way: there followed, Hazlitt says, 'those do-me-good, lack-a-daisical, whining, make-believe comedies in the next age, which are enough to set one to sleep, and where the author tries in vain to be merry and wise in the same breath.' These in place of 'the court, the gala day of wit and pleasure, of gallantry, and Charles the Second!' And all because people would not keep their functions distinct, and remember that as a comedy they were in a court of art and not in a court of law! The old comedy is dead, and its spirit gone from the stage: I have but endeavoured to show that no harm need come to our phylacteries, if a flame start from its ashes in the printed book.

II

William Congreve was born at Bardsey, near Leeds, and was baptized on 10th February 1670]. The Congreves were a Staffordshire family, of an antiquity of four hundred years at the date of the poet's birth. Richard, his grandfather, was a redoubtable Cavalier, and William, his father, an officer in the army. The latter was given a command at Youghal, while his son was still an infant, and becoming shortly afterwards agent to Lord Cork, removed to Lismore. So it chanced that the poet had his schooling at Kilkenny (with Swift), and proceeded to Trinity College, Dublin, in 1685, rejoining Swift, and like his friend becoming a pupil of St. George Ashe, the mathematician. In 1688 he left Dublin, remained with his people in Staffordshire for some two years, entered himself at the Temple, and came upon the town with The Old Bachelor in January 1692. The Double-Dealer was produced in November 1693. In 1694 a storm in the theatre led to a secession of Betterton and other renowned players from Drury Lane: with the result that a new playhouse was opened in Lincoln's Inn Fields, on 30th April 1695, with Love for Love. In the same year Congreve was appointed 'Commissioner for Licensing Hackney Coaches.' The Mourning Bride was produced in 1697, and was followed, oddly enough, by the controversy, or rather 'row,' with Jeremy Collier. In March 1700 came The Way of the World. The poet was made Commissioner of Wine-Licences in 1705, and in 1714 with his Jamaica secretaryship and his places in the Customs and the delightful 'Pipe-Office,' he had an income of twelve hundred pounds a year. He died at his house in Surrey Street, Strand, on 19th January 1729.

One or two comments on these dates are obvious. They dissipate the Thackerayan fable that on the production of The Old Bachelor, the fortunate young author received a shower of sinecures, 'all for writing a comedy.'

'And crazy Congreve scarce could spare
A shilling to discharge a chair,'

—writes Swift, and 'crazy' indicates that Congreve was gouty before he was rich. But then, the gout was a very early factor in his life, and one may call the line an exaggeration. Another couplet:

'Thus Congreve spent in writing plays,
And one poor office, half his days:'

—probably expresses the truth. With his plays and his hackney coaches he doubtless got through his twenties and thirties with no very hardly grinding poverty, and at forty or so was comfortably secure.

But another fact, which the dates bring out very sharply, has a different interest. At an age when Swift was beginning to try his powers, Congreve's work was done. A few odes, a few letters he was still to write, but no more comedies. Was it ill-health? or because the town had all but damned his greatest play? or because he cared more for life than for art?

III

The question brings one to an attempted appreciation of the man. Mr. Gosse, for whose Life I would express my gratitude, confesses that 'it is not very easy to construct a definite portrait of Congreve.' But that it baffled that very new journalist, Mrs. Manley, in his own day, and Mr. Gosse, with his information, in ours, to give 'salient points' to Congreve's character, proves in itself an essential characteristic, which need be negatively stated only by choice. That no amusing eccentricities are recorded, no ludicrous adventures, no persistent quarrels, implies, taken with other facts we know, that he was a well-bred man of the world, with the habit of society: that in itself is a definite personal quality. One supposes him an ease-loving man, not inclined to clown for the amusement of his world. He was loved by his friends, being tolerant, and understanding the art of social life. He was successful, and must therefore have had enemies, but he was careless to improve hostilities. For the temperament which is so plain in the best of his writings must have been present in his life—an unobtrusive, because a never directly implied, superiority and an ironical humour. The picture of swaggering snobbishness which Thackeray was inspired to make of him is proved bad by all that we know. A swaggerer could not have made a fast friend of Dryden—grown mellow, indeed, but by no means beggared of his fire—on his first coming to town, nor kept the intimacy of Swift, nor avoided the fault-finding of Dennis. It is quite unnecessary to suppose that Congreve's famous remark to Voltaire, that he wished to be visited as a plain gentleman, was the remark (if it was made) of a snob: it was clearly a legitimate deprecation, spoken by a man who had written nothing notable for twenty-six years, which Voltaire misunderstood in a moment of stupidity, or in one of forgetfulness misrepresented. His superiority and his irony came from a just sense of the perspective of things, and, not preventing affection for his friends, left him indifferent to his foes. Probably, also, a course of dissipation (at which Swift hints) in his youth, acting on a temperament not particularly ardent, had left him with such passions for war and love as were well under control. The two women with whom his name is connected were Mrs. Bracegirdle and the Duchess of Marlborough; but nobody knew—though the latter's mother hinted the worst—how far the intimacy went. That is to say, no patent scandal was necessary to the connexion, if in either case Congreve was a lover. And (once more) Congreve was a gentleman.

But why did he become sterile at thirty? Where, if not in dealing with motives and causes, may one be fancy-free? Here there are many, of which the first to be given is mere conjecture, but conjecture, I fancy, not inconsistent with such facts as are known. When Congreve produced his first comedy, he was but twenty-three, fresh from college and the country, ignorant, as we are told, of the world. He discovered very soon that he had an aptitude for social life, that, no doubt, living humours and follies were as entertaining as printed ones, that for a popular and witty man the world was pleasant. But no man may be socially finished all at once. In the course of the seven years between The Old Bachelor and The Way of the World, Congreve must have found his wit becoming readier, his tact surer, his appreciation of natural comedy finer and (as personal keenness decreased) more equable, his popularity greater, and—in fine—the world more pleasant and the attractions of the study waning and waning in comparison. He was a finished artist, he was born, one might almost say, with a style; but his inclination was to put his art into life rather than into print. Even in our days (thank God for all His mercies!) everybody is not writing a book. There are people whose talk has inimitable touches, and whose lives are art, but who never sit down to a quire of foolscap. I believe that Congreve naturally was one of these, that his literary ambition was a result of accidental necessity, and that had he lived as a boy in the society he was of as a very young man—for all its literary ornaments—we should have had of him only odes and songs. His generation was idler and took itself less seriously than ours. The primal curse was not imposed on everybody as a duty. In seven years of growing appreciation Congreve came to think the little graces and humours the better part. That I believe to have been the first cause of his early sterility; but others helped to determine the effect. A certain indolence is of course implied in what has been said. There was the gout, and there were his unfortunate obesity and his failing sight. There was Henrietta, Duchess of Marlborough, an absorbing dame. There were the success of Love for Love and the failure of The Way of the World. For all that may be said of the indifference of the true artist to the verdict of the many-headed beast—and Congreve's contempt was as fine as any—it is not amusing when your play or your book falls flat, and Congreve must have known that he might write another, and possibly a better, Way of the World, but no more Love for Loves. Not to anticipate a later division of the subject, it may be said here that a man of thirty, of a fine intellect and a fine taste, of a languid habit withal, and with an invalided constitution, while he might repeat the triumphs of diction and intellect of The Way of the World, was most unlikely to return to the broader humours and the more popular gaiety of the other play. Congreve, like Rochester before him, despised the judgment of the town in these matters, but by the town he would have to be judged.

He was a witty, handsome man of the world, of imperturbable temper and infinite tact, who could make and keep the friendship of very various men, and be intimate with a woman without quarrelling with her lovers. He had a taste for pictures and a love for music. He must have hated violence and uproar, and liked the finer shades of life. He wore the mode of his day, and was free from the superficial protests of the narrow-minded. Possibly not a very 'definite portrait,' possibly a very negative characterisation. Possibly, also, a tolerably sure foundation for a structure of sympathetic imagination.

IV

Passing from necessarily vague and not obviously pertinent remarks to criticism, which may fairly be less diffident, we leave Congreve's life and come to his work, to his 'tawdry playhouse taper,' as Thackeray called it. It is only after the man has appeared that we recognise that he came at the hour; but the nature of the hour is in this case not difficult to be discerned. The habit of playgoing was well-established; the turmoil of the Revolution was over; De Jure was at a comfortable distance, and De Facto's wife was a patroness of the arts. But playgoers had but to be shown something better than that they had, to discover that the convention of the Restoration needed new blood. A justification of its choice of material has been attempted: there is no inconsistency in affirming that the tendency to use it with a mere monotony of ribaldry was emphatic. Of this tendency the most notable and useful illustration is Wycherley, because in point of wit and dramatic skill he dwarfed his colleagues. As Mr. Swinburne has said, the art of Congreve is different in kind, not merely in degree, from the cruder and more boisterous product of the 'brawny' dramatist. Happily, however, for his success, the difference was not instantly clear. His first play links him with Wycherley, not with that rare and faint embryo of the later Congreve, George Etherege. 'You was always a gentleman, Mr. George,' as the valet says in Beau Austin. Happily for his popularity Congreve first followed the more popular man. It is not, indeed, until he wrote his last play that he was a whole Etherege idealised, albeit a greater than Etherege in the meantime. The peculiar effect which Etherege achieved in Sir Fopling Flutter—at whom and with whom you laugh at once—was not sublimated (the fineness left, the faintness become firmness) until Congreve created Witwoud, the inimitable, in The Way of the World.

At the very first Congreve had good fortune in his players. It was a brave time for them. True, their salaries were not wonderfully large. Colley Cibber complains of the days before the revolt in 1694: 'at what unequal salaries the hired actors were held by the absolute authority of their frugal masters, the patentees.' But the example was not faded of those gay days when they were the pets of the most artistic court that England has known: when great ladies carried Kynaston in his woman's dress to Hyde Park after the play, and the King was the most persistent and the most interested playgoer in his realm. They were not thus petted for irrelevant reasons—for their respectability, their piety, or their domestic virtues; and their recognition as artists by an artistic society did not spoil their art. When Congreve started on his course of play-writing, Queen Mary kept up, in a measure, the amiable custom of her uncle. He was very fortunate in his casts. There was Betterton, first of all, the versatile, the restrained, and, witness everybody, the incomparable. There was Underhill, 'a correct and natural comedian'—one must quote Cibber pretty often in this connexion—not well suited, one must suppose, to play Setter to Betterton's Heartwell in The Old Bachelor, but by reason of his admirable assumption of stupidity to make an excellent Sir Sampson in Love for Love. There were Powel, Williams, Verbruggen, Bowen, and Dogget (Fondlewife in the first play: afterwards Ben Legend, a part which made his fame and turned his head)—all notable comedians. Kynaston, graceful in old age as he had been beautiful in youth, was not in The Old Bachelor, but created Lord Touchwood in The Double-Dealer. Mountfort had been murdered by my Lord Mohun, and Leigh had followed him to the grave, but their names lived in their wives. Mrs. Mountfort 'was mistress of more variety of humour than I ever knew in any one woman actress . . . nothing, though ever so barren, if within the bounds of nature, could be flat in her hands.' Indeed 'she was so fond of humour, in what low part soever to be found, that she would make no scruple of defacing her fair form to come heartily into it'—assuredly a rare actress! About Mrs. Leigh Cibber is less enthusiastic, but grants her 'a good deal of humour': her old women were famous. Mrs. Barry was a stately, dignified actress, best, no doubt, in tragedy. Lastly, there was Mrs. Bracegirdle, the innocent publica cura, whom authors courted through their plays, and who had all the men in the house for longing lovers. Who shall say how far 'her youth and lively aspect' influenced the criticisms that have come down to us? She played Millamant to Congreve's satisfaction.

V

It is not difficult to understand how it was that Dryden thought The Old Bachelor the best first play he had seen, and the town applauded to the echo. But it is a little hard to understand why later critics, with the three other comedies before them, have not more expressly marked the difference between the first and those. There is no new tune in The Old Bachelor: it is an old tune more finely played, and for that very reason it met with immediate acceptance. It is not likely that Dryden—a great poet and a great and generous critic, it may be, but an old man—would have bestowed such unhesitating approval on a play which ignored the conventions in which he had lived. As it was, he saw those conventions reverently followed, yet served by a master wit. The fact that Congreve allowed Dryden and others to 'polish' his play, by giving it an air of the stage and the town which it lacked, need not of course spoil it for us. The stamp of Congreve is clearly marked on the dialogue, though not on every page. You may see its essentials in two passages taken absolutely at random. 'Come, come,' says Bellmour in the very first scene, 'leave business to idlers and wisdom to fools; they have need of 'em: wit be my faculty and pleasure my occupation, and let Father Time shake his glass.' Or Fondlewife soliloquises: 'Tell me, Isaac, why art thee jealous? Why art thee distrustful of the wife of thy bosom? Because she is young and vigorous, and I am old and impotent. Then why didst thee marry, Isaac? Because she was beautiful and tempting, and because I was obstinate and doating. . . .' In the one passage is the gay and skilfully light paradox, in the other the clean, rhythmical, and balanced, yet dramatic and appropriate English that are elements of Congreve's style. It is in the conventions of its characterisation that The Old Bachelor belongs, not to true Congrevean comedy but, to that of the models from which he was to break away. The characterisation of The Way of the World is light and true, that of The Old Bachelor is heavy and yet vague. Vainlove indeed, the 'mumper in love,' who 'lies canting at the gate,' is individual and Congrevean. But Heartwell, the blustering fool, Bellmour, the impersonal rake, Wittol and Bluffe, the farcical sticks, Fondlewife, the immemorial city husband, and the troop of undistinguished women— what can be said of them but that they are glaring stage properties, speaking better English than the comic stage had before attracted? Germs, possibly, of better things to come, that is all, so far as characterisation goes. The Fondlewife episode, in particular, which doubtless was mightily popular— what is there more in it than the mutton fisted wit and brutality of Wyeherley, with some of Congreve's English? Such scenes as these, it may be hazarded, so contemptible in the light of Congreve's better work, are ineffective now because they fall between two stools: between the comedy (or tragedy) of a crude physical fact, naked and impossible, as in Rochester, and the comedy (or tragedy) of delicately-phrased intrigue. The latter was yet to come when this play was produced, and meantime such episodes went very well, and their popularity is intelligible. For the rest The Old Bachelor, though to us in these days its plot appear a somewhat uninspiring piece of fairyland, was a good acting play, fitted with great skill to its actual players. The part of Fondlewife, created by Dogget, was on a revival played (to his own immense satisfaction) by Colley Cibber. In Araminta Mrs. Bracegirdle began (in a faint outline as it were) the series of lively, sympathetic, intelligent heroines which Congreve wrote for her. Lord Falkland's Prologue is as funny as it is indecently suggestive, which is saying a great deal. The one actually spoken gave an opportunity of the merriest archness to Mrs. Bracegirdle, and was calculated to put the audience in the best of good humours.

The faults of The Double-Dealer are obvious on a first reading, and were very justly condemned on a first acting. The intrigue is wearisome: its involutions are ineffectively puzzling. Maskwell's villainy and Mellefont's folly are both unconvincing. The tragedy of Lady Touchwood, less tragic than that of Lady Wishfort in The Way of the World, is more obviously than that out of the picture. The play is, in fact, not pure comedy of manners: it is that plus tragedy, an element less offensive than the sentimentality which spoils The School for Scandal, but yet a notable fault. For while you can resolve the tragedy of Lady Wishfort into wicked and very grim comedy, you can do nothing with the tragedy of Lady Touchwood but try to ignore it. In his epistle dedicatory to Charles Montague, Congreve admits that his play has faults, but does not take in hand those adduced above, with the exception of the objections to Maskwell and Mellefont. 'They have mistaken cunning in one character for folly in another': an ineffectual answer, because the extremity of cunning is equally destructive of dramatic balance. He defends his use of soliloquy very warmly: of which it may be said that, so long as his rule—that no character may overhear the soliloquiser—is observed, it is a tolerable convention, but a confession of weakness in construction. He declares he 'would rather disoblige all the critics in the world than one of the fair sex,' and, having made his bow, he turns upon the ladies and rends them. An author campaigning against his critics is always a pleasant spectacle, but Congreve's defence of The Double-Dealer is rather amusing than convincing.

It needed no defence; for with all its faults, such as they are, upon it, there are in it scenes and characters which only Congreve could have made. Brisk is a worthy forerunner of Witwoud, Sir Paul Plyant a delicious old credulous fool; while the tyrannical and vain Lady Plyant is so drawn that you almost love her. But the triumph is Lady Froth, 'a great coquet, pretender to poetry, wit, and learning,' and one would almost as lief have seen Mrs. Mountfort in the part as the Bracegirdle's Millamant. Her serious folly and foolish wisdom, her poem and malice and compliments and babbling vivacity—set off, it is fair to remember, by a pretty face—are atonement for a dozen Maskwells. She is a female Witwoud, her author's first success in a sort of character he draws to perfection. The scene between Mellefont and Lady Plyant, where she insists on believing that the gallant, under cover of a marriage with her stepdaughter, purposes to lead her astray, and where she goes through a delightful farce of answering her scruples before the bewildered man—the scene that for some far-fetched reason led Macaulay's mind to the incest in the Oedipus Rex—is perhaps the best comedy of situation in the piece. But the scene of defamation between the Froths and Brisk is notable as (with the Cabal idea in The Way of the World) the inspiration of the Scandal Scenes in Sheridan's play. When we remember that less than two years were gone since the production of The Old Bachelor, the improvement in Congreve is remarkable. Almost his only concession to the groundlings is the star-gazing episode of Lady Froth and Brisk: a mistake, because it spoils her inconsequent folly, but a small matter. In his second play Congreve was himself, the wittiest and most polished writer of comedy in English. In the face of this fact 'the public' conducted itself characteristically: it more or less damned The Double-Dealer until the queen approved, when it applauded lustily. That occasion gave Colley Cibber his first chance as Kynaston's substitute in Lord Touchwood. When one remembers Dryden's long, struggling, cudgelling and cudgelled life, it is impossible to read without emotion his tribute to a very young and successful author in the verses prefixed to this play:

Firm Doric pillars found your solid base: The fair Corinthian crowns the higher space; Thus all below is strength, and all above is grace. . . . . . We cannot envy you, because we love. . . . . . Time, place, and action may with pains be wrought, But Genius must be born, and never can be taught. This is your portion, this your native store; Heav'n, that but once was prodigal before. To Shakespeare gave as much; she could not give him more.

The tribute is indubitably sincere; in point of Congreve's wit and diction it is as indubitably true.

Love for Love was the most popular of Congreve's comedies: it held the stage so long that Hazlitt could say, 'it still acts and is still acted well.' Being wise after the event, one may give some obvious reasons. It is more human than any other of his plays, and at the same time more farcical. By 'more human' it is not meant that the characters are truer to life than those in The Way of the World, but that they are truer to average life, and therefore more easily recognisable by the average spectator. Tattle, for instance, is so gross a fool, that any fool in the pit could see his folly; Witwoud might deceive all but the elect. No familiarity—direct or indirect—with a particular mode of life and speech is necessary to the appreciation of Love for Love. Sir Sampson Legend is your unmistakable heavy father, cross-grained and bullying. Valentine is no ironical, fine gentleman like Mirabell, but a young rake from Cambridge, all debts and high spirits. Scandal is a plain railer at things, especially women; Ben Legend a sea-dog who cannot speak without a nautical metaphor; Jeremy an idealised comic servant; and Foresight grotesque farce. Angelica is a shrewd but hearty 'English girl,' and Miss Prue a veritable country Miss; while Mrs. Frail and Mrs. Foresight are broadly skittish matrons. There is nothing in the play to strain the attention or to puzzle the intellect, and it is full of laughter: no wonder it was a success. It is, intellectually, on an altogether different plane from The Way of the World, on a slightly lower one than The Double-Dealer. But in its own way it is irresistibly funny, and by reason of its diction it is never for a moment other than distinguished.

I imagine the bodkin scene will always take the palm in it for mere mirth. Delightful sisters!

I suppose you would not go alone to the World's End?

The World's End! What, do you mean to banter me?

Poor innocent! You don't know that there's a place called the World's End?

I'll swear you can keep your countenance purely; you'd make an admirable player. . . . But look you here, now—where did you lose this gold bodkin?—Oh, sister, sister!

My bodkin?

Nay, 'tis yours; look at it.

Well, if you go to that, where did you find this bodkin? Oh, sister, sister!—sister every way.

Broad, popular comedy, it is admirable; but it is not especially Congrevean. Tattle's love-lesson to Miss Prue and his boasting of his duchesses are in the same broad vein. Valentine's mad scene is more remarkable, in that Congreve gives rein to his fancy, and that his diction is at its very best. 'Hark'ee, I have a secret to tell you. Endymion and the Moon shall meet us upon Mount Latmos, and will be married in the dead of night. But say not a word. Hymen shall put his torch into a dark lanthorn, that it may be secret, and Juno shall give her peacock poppy-water, that he may fold his ogling tail, and Argus's hundred eyes be shut, ha? Nobody shall know, but Jeremy.'

TATTLE
O you know me, Valentine?

VALENTINE
You? Who are you? No, I hope not.

TATTLE
I am Jack Tattle, your friend.

VALENTINE
My friend, what to do? I am no married man, and thou canst not lie with my wife. I am very poor, and thou canst not borrow money of me. Then, what employment have I for a friend?

ANGELICA
Do you know me, Valentine?

VALENTINE
Oh, very well.

ANGELICA
Who am I?

VALENTINE
You're a woman, one to whom Heaven gave beauty when it grafted roses on a briar. You are the reflection of Heaven in a pond, and he that leaps at you is sunk. You are all white, a sheet of lovely, spotless paper, when you first are born; but you are to be scrawled and blotted by every goose's quill. I

know you; for I loved a woman, and loved her so long, that I found out a strange thing: I found out what a woman was good for.

Imagine Betterton, the greatest actor of his time, delivering that last speech, with its incomparable rhythm! I like to think that he gave the spectators an idea that Valentine's self-sacrifice for Angelica was nothing but a bold device, a calculated effect; otherwise the sacrifice is an excrescence in this comedy, which, popular and broad though it be, is cynical in Congreve's manner throughout. One is consoled, however, by the pleasant fate of the ingenious Mr. Tattle and the intriguing Mrs. Frail, who are left tied for life against their will. The trick, by the way, of a tricked marriage is constant in Congreve, and reveals his poverty of construction. He can devise you comic situations unflaggingly, but when he approaches the end of a play his deus ex machinâ is invariably this flattest and most battered old deity in fairyland.

The dedication to Lord Dorset contains nothing of interest beyond the confession that the play is too long, and the information that part of it was omitted in the playing. A line in the prologue, 'We grieve One falling Adam and one tempted Eve,' is explained by Colley Cibber to refer to Mrs. Mountford, who, having cast her lot with Betterton and migrated to Lincoln's Inn Fields, threw up her part on a question of cash, and to Williams, an actor who 'loved his bottle better than his business,' who deserted at the same time. It serves to show the interest the town took in the players, that the fact was referred to on the stage. The lady's part was taken by Mrs. Ayliff; Mrs. Leigh played the nurse—a very poor part after Lady Plyant; Dogget's success as Ben Legend has been noted. Mrs. Bracegirdle's Angelica was doubtless ravishing: a 'virtuous young woman,' as our ancestors phrased it, but quite relieved from insipidity.

It would need a greater presumption than the writer is gifted withal to add his contribution to the praises critics have lavished on The Way of the World. It is better to quote Mr. Swinburne. 'In 1700 Congreve replied to Collier with the crowning work of his genius—the unequalled and unapproached masterpiece of English comedy. The one play in our language which may fairly claim a place beside, or but just beneath, the mightiest work of Molière, is The Way of the World.' But he continues: 'On the stage, which had recently acclaimed with uncritical applause the author's more questionable appearance in the field of tragedy,'—The Mourning Bride,—'this final and flawless evidence of his incomparable powers met with a rejection then and ever since inexplicable on any ground of conjecture.' There the critics are not unanimous. Mr. Gosse, for instance, has his explanation: that the spectators must have fidgeted, and wished 'that the actors and actresses would be doing something.' Very like, indeed: the spectators, then as now, would no doubt have preferred 'knock-about farce.' But, I venture to think, the explanation is not complete. The construction of the play is weak, certainly, but the actors and actresses do a great deal after all. For that matter, audiences will stand scenes of still wit— but they like to comprehend it; and the characters in The Way of the World, or most of them, represent a society whose attitude and speech are entirely ironical and paradoxical, a society of necessity but a small fraction of any community. Some sort of study or some special experience is necessary to the enjoyment of such a set. It is not the case of a few witticisms and paradoxes firing off at intervals, like crackers, from the mouths of one or two actors with whom the audience is taught to laugh as a matter of course: the vein is unbroken. Now, literalness and common sense are the qualities of the average uninstructed spectator, and The Way of the World was high over the heads of its audience.

To come to details. The tragedy of Lady Wishfort has often been remarked—the veritable tragedy of a lovesick old woman. All the grotesque touches, her credulity, her vanity, her admirable dialect ('as I'm a person!'), but serve to make the tragedy the more pitiable. Either, therefore, our appreciation of satiric comedy is defective, or Congreve made a mistake. To regard this poor old soul as mere comedy is to attain to an almost satanic height of contempt: the comedy is more than grim, it is savagely cruel. To be pitiless, on the other hand, is a satirist's virtue. On the whole, we may reasonably say that the tragedy is not too keen in itself, but that it is too obviously indicated. Witwoud is surely a great character? The stage is alive with mirth when he is on it. His entrance in the very first part of the play is delightful. 'Afford me your compassion, my dears; pity me, Fainall; Mirabell, pity me. . . . Fainall, how does your lady? Gad, I say anything in the world to get this fellow out of my head. I beg pardon that I should ask a man of pleasure, and the town, a question at once so foreign and domestic. But I talk like an old maid at a marriage, I don't know what I say.' But one might quote for ever. Witwoud, almost as much as Millamant herself, is an eternal type. His little exclamations, his assurance of sympathy, his terror of the commonplace—surely one knows them well? His tolerance of any impertinence, lest he should be thought to have misunderstood a jest, is a great distinction. But Congreve's gibe in the dedication at the critics, who failed 'to distinguish betwixt the character of a Witwoud and a Truewit,' is hardly fair: as Dryden said of Etherege's Sir Fopling, he is 'a fool so nicely writ, The ladies might mistake him for a wit.' Then, Millamant is the ultimate expression of those who, having all the material goods which nature and civilisation can give, live on paradoxes and artifices. Her insolence is the inoffensive insolence only possible to the well-bred. 'O ay, letters,—I had letters,—I am persecuted with letters,—I hate letters,—nobody knows how to write letters; and yet one has 'em, one does not know why,—they serve one to pin up one's hair.' 'Beauty the lover's gift!—Lord, what is a lover, that it can give? Why one makes lovers as fast as one pleases, and they live as long as one pleases, and they die as soon as one pleases; and then if one pleases one makes more.'

In parts of its characterisation The Way of the World is extremely bold in observation, extremely careless of literary types and traditions. Mrs. Fainall, a woman who is the friend, and assists in the intrigues, of a man who has ceased to be her lover, is most unconventionally human. Of all the inimitable scenes, that in which Millamant and Mirabell make their conditions of marriage is perhaps the most unquestionable triumph. 'Let us never visit together, nor go to a play together, but let us be very strange and well-bred'—there is its keynote. The dialogue is as sure and perfect in diction, in balance of phrases, and in musical effectiveness as can be conceived, and for all its care is absolutely free in its gaiety. It is the ultimate expression of the joys of the artificial. As for the prologue, it is an invitation to the dullards to damn the play, and is anything but serenely confident. The dedication, to 'Ralph, Earl of Mountague,' has an interesting fact: it tells us that the comedy was written immediately after staying with him, 'in your retirement last summer from the town,' and pays a tribute to the influence of the society the dramatist met there. 'Vous y voyez partout,' said Voltaire of Congreve, 'le langage des honnêtes gens avec des actions de fripon; ce qui prouve qu'il connaissait bien son monde, et qu'il vivait dans ce qu'on appelle la bonne compagnie.'

The want of dramatic skill which has been alleged against Congreve is simply a question of construction—of the construction of his plays as a whole. His plots hang fire, are difficult to follow, and are not worth remembering. But many things besides go to the making of good plays, and few playwrights have had all the theatrical virtues. Do we not pardon a lack of incident in a novel of character? In this connexion it is worth while to contrast Congreve with Sheridan, who in the matter of construction was a far abler craftsman. But is there not in the elder poet enough to turn the scale, even the theatrical scale, ten times over? Compare the petty indignation, with which the dramatist of The School for Scandal deals with his scandalmongers, and the amused indifference of Congreve towards the cabalists in The Way of the World. Or take any hero of Congreve's and contrast him with that glorification of vulgar lavishness and canting generosity, that very barmaid's hero, Charles Surface. It is all very well to say that Joseph is the real hero; but Sheridan made it natural for the stupid sentimentality of later days to make him the villain, and Congreve would have made it impossible. Of wit (of course) there is more in a scene of Congreve than in a play of Sheridan. Moreover, faulty in construction as his main plots are, in detail his construction is often admirable: as in play of character upon character, in countless opportunities for delightful archness and cruelty in the women, for the display of every comic emotion in the men. He lived in the playhouse, and his characters, true to life though they be, have about them as it were an ideal essence of the boards. With Hazlitt, 'I would rather have seen Mrs. Abington's Millamant than any Rosalind that ever appeared on the stage.' A lover and a constant frequenter of the theatre—albeit the plays he sees bore him to death—cannot, in reading Congreve, choose but see the glances and hear the intonations of imaginary players.

VI

Congreve's choice of material has been defended at an early stage of these remarks. There is the further and more interesting question of his point of view, his attitude towards it. Mr. Henley speaks of his 'deliberate and unmitigable baseness of morality.' Differing with deference, I think it may be shown that his attitude is a pose merely, and an artistic and quite innocent pose. It is the amusing pose of the boyish cynic turned into an artistic convention. The lines:

'He alone won't betray in whom none will confide,
And the nymph may be chaste that has never been tried:'

—which conclude the characteristic song in the third act of Love for Love, are typical of his attitude. Does anybody suppose that an intelligent man of the world meant that sentiment in all seriousness?

'Nothing's new besides our faces,
Every woman is the same'—

—those lines (in his first play), which seemed so shocking to Thackeray, what more do they express than the green cynicism of youth? When Mr. Leslie Stephen speaks of his 'gush of cynical sentiment,' he speaks unsympathetically, but the phrase, to be an enemy's, is just. It is cynical sentiment, and the hostility comes from taking it seriously. I think it the most artistic attitude for a writer of gay, satiric comedies, and that its very excess should prevent its being taken for more than a convention. We are not called upon to see satiric comedies all day long, and the question, everlastingly asked by implication of every work of art—'Would you like to live with it?'—is here, as in most other cases, irrelevant. One is reminded that there is more in life than intrigues and cynical comments on them. And one is inclined to put the questions in answer: 'Does a man who really feels the sorrowful things of life, its futile endeavours and piteous separations, find relief in seeing his emotions mimicked on the stage in a 'wholesome' play of sentiment with a happy ending? Is he not rather comforted by the distractions of cheerful frivolity, of conventional denial of his pains?' The demand is as inartistic and irrelevant as the criticism which suggested it, but it returns a sufficient reply. It does not touch the 'catharsis' of tragedy, which is another matter. For the rest, Congreve's attitude, cynicism apart, is an attitude of irony and superiority over common emotions, the attitude, artificial and inoffensive, of the society he depicts in his greatest play. He enjoys the humours of his puppets, he is never angry with them. It is the attitude of an artist in expounding human nature, of an expert in observation of life: an attitude attainable but by very few, and disliked as a rule by the rest, who want to clap or to hiss—who can laugh but who cannot smile.

VII

When Congreve left the stage, said Dennis the critic, 'comedy left it with him.' Vanburgh and Farquhar were left to expound comedy of manners, the one with a vigorous gusto, the other with a romantic gaiety. The peculiar perfume of The Way of the World was given to neither, yet they wrote comedy of manners. But if Congreve left colleagues, he left no sons, and most certainly, one may say, that when those colleagues died, English comedy took to her bed. 'The Comic Muse, long sick, is now a-dying,' wrote Garrick in his prologue to She Stoops to Conquer, and she had not to apologise, like Charles the Second, for the unconscionable time she was about it. It is a little crude to attribute her demise to Jeremy Collier and his Short View—a block painted to look like a thunderbolt. It is not a matter of decency, of alteration or improvement in manners. A comedy might be wholly Congrevean without a coarse word from beginning to end. It is a matter of the exclusion (not the stultification), the suspension of moral prepossessions, the absence of sympathetic sentimentalism, the habit of shirking nothing and smiling at all things. These qualities are not characteristic of the average Englishman. Now, satiric comedy did not in its initiation depend upon the average Englishman. It took its cue from the court of Charles the Second, who—with a dash of thoroughly English humour—was more than half-French in temperament, and attracted to himself all that was artistically frivolous in his kingdom. Questions of decency and morality—which after all are not perpetually amusing—apart, the social spirit typified in this exceptional king is one of sceptical humour and ironical smiles: it takes common emotions for granted—is bored by them, in fact—and is a foe to sentimentality and gush and virtuously happy endings. It was the spirit of Charles the Second that inspired English comedy, and inspired it most thoroughly in Congreve but a few years after Charles's death. Under changed conditions, one is apt to underestimate the influence of the Court upon the Town two hundred years ago. Well, the Georges became our defenders of the faith, and they hated 'boets and bainters.' English comedy was thrown back upon the patronage and the inspiration of average England, and up to the time of writing has shown few signs of recovery. Of course, the decay was gradual: you may see it at a most interesting stage in The School for Scandal, a comedy of manners with a strong dash of common sentimentality. It would be just possible, one conceives, to play The School for Scandal as Charles Lamb says he saw it played, with Joseph for a hero, as a comedy of manners: you can just imagine Sir Peter as a sort of Sir Paul Plyant, and as not played to raise a lump in your throat. But Sheridan made it a difficult task. Perhaps you may see the evil influence at its worst in the so-called comedies which were our glory twenty-five years ago: in such a play as Caste, an even river of sloppy sentiment, where the acme of chivalrous delicacy is to refrain from lighting a cigarette in a woman's presence, where the triumph of humour is for a guardsman to take a kettle off the fire, and where the character of Eccles shows what excellent comedy the author might (alas!) have written.

One is fain to ask if the spirit of Congrevean comedy will ever come back to our stage. An echo of it has been heard in dialogue once or twice in the last few years: not a trace has been seen in action. And yet we permit our dramatists a pretty wide range of subjects. We allow the subjects: it is the Congrevean attitude towards them which we should condemn. But the stage would be all the merrier if we could only understand that that attitude is harmless; that to see the humorous aspect of a thing is not to ignore the pathetic or the sociological; and that we should return all the heartier to our serious and sentimental considerations of the problems of life for allowing them to be laughed at for an evening at a comedy. Meantime we can read the book.

G. S. STREET.

THE OLD BACHELOR: A COMEDY

Quem tulit ad scenam ventoso Gloria curru, Exanimat lentus spectator; sedulus inflat: Sic leve, sic parvum est, animum quod laudis avarum Subruit, and reficit.

—HORAT. Epist. I. lib. ii.

TO THE RIGHT HONOURABLE CHARLES, LORD CLIFFORD OF LANESBOROUGH, ETC.

My Lord,—It is with a great deal of pleasure that I lay hold on this first occasion which the accidents of my life have given me of writing to your lordship: for since at the same time I write to all the world, it will be a means of publishing (what I would have everybody know) the respect and duty which I owe and pay to you. I have so much inclination to be yours that I need no other engagement. But the particular ties by which I am bound to your lordship and family have put it out of my power to make you any compliment, since all offers of myself will amount to no more than an honest acknowledgment, and only shew a willingness in me to be grateful.

I am very near wishing that it were not so much my interest to be your lordship's servant, that it might be more my merit; not that I would avoid being obliged to you, but I would have my own choice to run me into the debt: that I might have it to boast, I had distinguished a man to whom I would be glad to be obliged, even without the hopes of having it in my power ever to make him a return.

It is impossible for me to come near your lordship in any kind and not to receive some favour; and while in appearance I am only making an acknowledgment (with the usual underhand dealing of the world) I am at the same time insinuating my own interest. I cannot give your lordship your due, without tacking a bill of my own privileges. 'Tis true, if a man never committed a folly, he would never stand in need of a protection. But then power would have nothing to do, and good nature no occasion to show itself; and where those qualities are, 'tis pity they should want objects to shine upon. I must confess this is no reason why a man should do an idle thing, nor indeed any good excuse for it when done; yet it reconciles the uses of such authority and goodness to the necessities of our follies, and is a sort of poetical logic, which at this time I would make use of, to argue your lordship into a protection of this play. It is the first offence I have committed in this kind, or indeed, in any kind of poetry, though not the first made public, and therefore I hope will the more easily be pardoned. But had it been acted, when it was first written, more might have been said in its behalf: ignorance of the town and stage would then have been excuses in a young writer, which now almost four years' experience will scarce allow of. Yet I must declare myself sensible of the good nature of the town, in receiving this play so kindly, with all its faults, which I must own were, for the most part, very industriously covered by the care of the players; for I think scarce a character but received all the advantage it would admit of from the justness of the action.

As for the critics, my lord, I have nothing to say to, or against, any of them of any kind: from those who make just exceptions, to those who find fault in the wrong place. I will only make this general answer in behalf of my play (an answer which Epictetus advises every man to make for himself to his censurers), viz.: 'That if they who find some faults in it, were as intimate with it as I am, they would find a great many more.' This is a confession, which I needed not to have made; but however, I can draw this use from it to my own advantage: that I think there are no faults in it but what I do know; which, as I take it, is the first step to an amendment.

Thus I may live in hopes (sometime or other) of making the town amends; but you, my lord, I never can, though I am ever your lordship's most obedient and most humble servant,

WILL. CONGREVE.

TO MR. CONGREVE.

When virtue in pursuit of fame appears,
And forward shoots the growth beyond the years.
We timely court the rising hero's cause,
And on his side the poet wisely draws,
Bespeaking him hereafter by applause.
The days will come, when we shall all receive
Returning interest from what now we give,
Instructed and supported by that praise
And reputation which we strive to raise.
Nature so coy, so hardly to be wooed,
Flies, like a mistress, but to be pursued.
O Congreve! boldly follow on the chase:
She looks behind and wants thy strong embrace:
She yields, she yields, surrenders all her charms,
Do you but force her gently to your arms:
Such nerves, such graces, in your lines appear,
As you were made to be her ravisher.
Dryden has long extended his command,
By right divine, quite through the muses' land,
Absolute lord; and holding now from none,
But great Apollo, his undoubted crown.
That empire settled, and grown old in power
Can wish for nothing but a successor:
Not to enlarge his limits, but maintain
Those provinces, which he alone could gain.
His eldest Wycherly, in wise retreat,
Thought it not worth his quiet to be great.
Loose, wand'ring Etherege, in wild pleasures tost,
And foreign int'rests, to his hopes long lost:
Poor Lee and Otway dead! Congreve appears,
The darling, and last comfort of his years.
May'st thou live long in thy great master's smiles,
And growing under him, adorn these isles.
But when—when part of him, be that but late
His body yielding must submit to fate,
Leaving his deathless works and thee behind

(The natural successor of his mind),
Then may'st thou finish what he has begun:
Heir to his merit, be in fame his son.
What thou hast done, shews all is in thy pow'r,
And to write better, only must write more.
'Tis something to be willing to commend;
But my best praise is, that I am your friend,

THO. SOUTHERNE.

TO MR. CONGREVE.

The danger's great in these censorious days,
When critics are so rife to venture praise:
When the infectious and ill-natured brood
Behold, and damn the work, because 'tis good,
And with a proud, ungenerous spirit, try
To pass an ostracism on poetry.
But you, my friend, your worth does safely bear
Above their spleen; you have no cause for fear;
Like a well-mettled hawk, you took your flight
Quite out of reach, and almost out of sight.
As the strong sun, in a fair summer's day,
You rise, and drive the mists and clouds away,
The owls and bats, and all the birds of prey.
Each line of yours, like polished steel's so hard,
In beauty safe, it wants no other guard.
Nature herself's beholden to your dress,
Which though still like, much fairer you express.
Some vainly striving honour to obtain,
Leave to their heirs the traffic of their brain:
Like China under ground, the ripening ware,
In a long time, perhaps grows worth our care.
But you now reap the fame, so well you've sown;
The planter tastes his fruit to ripeness grown.
As a fair orange-tree at once is seen
Big with what's ripe, yet springing still with green,
So at one time, my worthy friend appears,
With all the sap of youth, and weight of years.
Accept my pious love, as forward zeal,
Which though it ruins me I can't conceal:
Exposed to censure for my weak applause,
I'm pleased to suffer in so just a cause;
And though my offering may unworthy prove,
Take, as a friend, the wishes of my love.

J. MARSH.

Wit, like true gold, refined from all allay,
Immortal is, and never can decay:
'Tis in all times and languages the same,
Nor can an ill translation quench the flame:
For, though the form and fashion don't remain,
The intrinsic value still it will retain.
Then let each studied scene be writ with art,
And judgment sweat to form the laboured part.
Each character be just, and nature seem:
Without th' ingredient, wit, 'tis all but phlegm:
For that's the soul, which all the mass must move,
And wake our passions into grief or love.
But you, too bounteous, sow your wit so thick,
We are surprised, and know not where to pick;
And while with clapping we are just to you,
Ourselves we injure, and lose something new.
What mayn't we then, great youth, of thee presage,
Whose art and wit so much transcend thy age?
How wilt thou shine at thy meridian height,
Who, at thy rising, giv'st so vast a light?
When Dryden dying shall the world deceive,
Whom we immortal, as his works, believe,
Thou shalt succeed, the glory of the stage,
Adorn and entertain the coming age.

BEVIL. HIGGONS.

DRAMATIS PERSONÆ.

MEN

HEARTWELL, BELLMOUR
VAINLOVE
ARAMINTA
SHARPER
SIR JOSEPH WITTOL
CAPTAIN BLUFFE
FONDLEWIFE
SETTER
SERVANT

WOMEN

ARAMINTA
BELINDA
LÆTITIASYLVIALUCY
BETTY
BOY
FOOTMEN

PROLOGUE INTENDED FOR THE OLD BACHELOR. Written by the LORD FALKLAND.

Most authors on the stage at first appear
Like widows' bridegrooms, full of doubt and fear:
They judge, from the experience of the dame,
How hard a task it is to quench her flame;
And who falls short of furnishing a course
Up to his brawny predecessor's force,
With utmost rage from her embraces thrown,
Remains convicted as an empty drone.
Thus often, to his shame, a pert beginner
Proves in the end a miserable sinner.
As for our youngster, I am apt to doubt him,
With all the vigour of his youth about him;
But he, more sanguine, trusts in one and twenty,
And impudently hopes he shall content you:
For though his bachelor be worn and cold,
He thinks the young may club to help the old,
And what alone can be achieved by neither,
Is often brought about by both together.
The briskest of you all have felt alarms,
Finding the fair one prostitute her charms
With broken sighs, in her old fumbler's arms:
But for our spark, he swears he'll ne'er be jealous
Of any rivals, but young lusty fellows.
Faith, let him try his chance, and if the slave,
After his bragging, prove a washy knave,
May he be banished to some lonely den
And never more have leave to dip his pen.
But if he be the champion he pretends,
Both sexes sure will join to be his friends,
For all agree, where all can have their ends.
And you must own him for a man of might,
If he holds out to please you the third night.

PROLOGUE. Spoken by MRS. BRACEGIRDLE.

How this vile world is changed! In former days
Prologues were serious speeches before plays,
Grave, solemn things, as graces are to feasts,
Where poets begged a blessing from their guests.
But now no more like suppliants we come;
A play makes war, and prologue is the drum.
Armed with keen satire and with pointed wit,
We threaten you who do for judges sit,
To save our plays, or else we'll damn your pit.
But for your comfort, it falls out to-day,
We've a young author and his first-born play;
So, standing only on his good behaviour,
He's very civil, and entreats your favour.
Not but the man has malice, would he show it,
But on my conscience he's a bashful poet;
You think that strange—no matter, he'll outgrow it.
Well, I'm his advocate: by me he prays you
(I don't know whether I shall speak to please you),
He prays—O bless me! what shall I do now?
Hang me if I know what he prays, or how!
And 'twas the prettiest prologue as he wrote it!
Well, the deuce take me, if I han't forgot it.
O Lord, for heav'n's sake excuse the play,
Because, you know, if it be damned to-day,
I shall be hanged for wanting what to say.
For my sake then—but I'm in such confusion,
I cannot stay to hear your resolution.

[Runs off.]

SCENE: The Street.

ACT I

SCENE I

BELLMOUR and **VAINLOVE** meeting.

BELLMOUR

Vainlove, and abroad so early! Good-morrow; I thought a contemplative lover could no more have parted with his bed in a morning than he could have slept in't.

VAINLOVE

Bellmour, good-morrow. Why, truth on't is, these early sallies are not usual to me; but business, as you see, sir—

[Showing Letters.]

And business must be followed, or be lost.

BELLMOUR
Business! And so must time, my friend, be close pursued, or lost. Business is the rub of life, perverts our aim, casts off the bias, and leaves us wide and short of the intended mark.

VAINLOVE
Pleasure, I guess you mean.

BELLMOUR
Ay; what else has meaning?

VAINLOVE
Oh, the wise will tell you—

BELLMOUR
More than they believe—or understand.

VAINLOVE
How, how, Ned! A wise man say more than he understands?

BELLMOUR
Ay, ay! Wisdom's nothing but a pretending to know and believe more than we really do. You read of but one wise man, and all that he knew was, that he knew nothing. Come, come, leave business to idlers and wisdom to fools; they have need of 'em. Wit be my faculty, and pleasure my occupation; and let Father Time shake his glass. Let low and earthly souls grovel till they have worked themselves six foot deep into a grave. Business is not my element—I roll in a higher orb, and dwell—

VAINLOVE
In castles i' th' air of thy own building. That's thy element, Ned. Well, as high a flier as you are, I have a lure may make you stoop.

[Flings a Letter.]

BELLMOUR
I, marry, sir, I have a hawk's eye at a woman's hand. There's more elegancy in the false spelling of this superscription—

[Takes up the Letter]

—than in all Cicero. Let me see.—How now!—Dear perfidious Vainlove.

[Reads.]

VAINLOVE

Hold, hold, 'slife, that's the wrong.

BELLMOUR

Nay, let's see the name—Sylvia!—how canst thou be ungrateful to that creature? She's extremely pretty, and loves thee entirely—I have heard her breathe such raptures about thee—

VAINLOVE

Ay, or anybody that she's about—

BELLMOUR

No, faith, Frank, you wrong her; she has been just to you.

VAINLOVE

That's pleasant, by my troth, from thee, who hast had her.

BELLMOUR

Never—her affections. 'Tis true, by heaven: she owned it to my face; and, blushing like the virgin morn when it disclosed the cheat which that trusty bawd of nature, night, had hid, confessed her soul was true to you; though I by treachery had stolen the bliss.

VAINLOVE

So was true as turtle—in imagination—Ned, ha? Preach this doctrine to husbands, and the married women will adore thee.

BELLMOUR

Why, faith, I think it will do well enough, if the husband be out of the way, for the wife to show her fondness and impatience of his absence by choosing a lover as like him as she can; and what is unlike, she may help out with her own fancy.

VAINLOVE

But is it not an abuse to the lover to be made a blind of?

BELLMOUR

As you say, the abuse is to the lover, not the husband. For 'tis an argument of her great zeal towards him, that she will enjoy him in effigy.

VAINLOVE

It must be a very superstitious country where such zeal passes for true devotion. I doubt it will be damned by all our Protestant husbands for flat idolatry. But, if you can make Alderman Fondlewife of your persuasion, this letter will be needless.

BELLMOUR

What! The old banker with the handsome wife?

VAINLOVE

Ay.

BELLMOUR

Let me see—Lætitia! Oh, 'tis a delicious morsel. Dear Frank, thou art the truest friend in the world.

VAINLOVE

Ay, am I not? To be continually starting of hares for you to course. We were certainly cut out for one another; for my temper quits an amour just where thine takes it up. But read that; it is an appointment for me, this evening—when Fondlewife will be gone out of town, to meet the master of a ship, about the return of a venture which he's in danger of losing. Read, read.

BELLMOUR [Reads.]

Hum, Hum—Out of town this evening, and talks of sending for Mr. Spintext to keep me company; but I'll take care he shall not be at home. Good! Spintext! Oh, the fanatic one-eyed parson!

VAINLOVE

Ay.

BELLMOUR [Reads.]

Hum, Hum—That your conversation will be much more agreeable, if you can counterfeit his habit to blind the servants. Very good! Then I must be disguised?—With all my heart!—It adds a gusto to an amour; gives it the greater resemblance of theft; and, among us lewd mortals, the deeper the sin the sweeter. Frank, I'm amazed at thy good nature—

VAINLOVE

Faith, I hate love when 'tis forced upon a man, as I do wine. And this business is none of my seeking; I only happened to be, once or twice, where Lætitia was the handsomest woman in company; so, consequently, applied myself to her—and it seems she has taken me at my word. Had you been there, or anybody, 't had been the same.

BELLMOUR

I wish I may succeed as the same.

VAINLOVE

Never doubt it; for if the spirit of cuckoldom be once raised up in a woman, the devil can't lay it, until she has done't.

BELLMOUR

Prithee, what sort of fellow is Fondlewife?

VAINLOVE

A kind of mongrel zealot, sometimes very precise and peevish. But I have seen him pleasant enough in his way; much addicted to jealousy, but more to fondness; so that as he is often jealous without a cause, he's as often satisfied without reason.

BELLMOUR

A very even temper, and fit for my purpose. I must get your man Setter to provide my disguise.

VAINLOVE

Ay; you may take him for good and all, if you will, for you have made him fit for nobody else. Well—

BELLMOUR

You're going to visit in return of Sylvia's letter. Poor rogue! Any hour of the day or night will serve her. But do you know nothing of a new rival there?

VAINLOVE

Yes; Heartwell—that surly, old, pretended woman-hater—thinks her virtuous; that's one reason why I fail her. I would have her fret herself out of conceit with me, that she may entertain some thoughts of him. I know he visits her every day.

BELLMOUR

Yet rails on still, and thinks his love unknown to us. A little time will swell him so, he must be forced to give it birth; and the discovery must needs be very pleasant from himself, to see what pains he will take, and how he will strain to be delivered of a secret, when he has miscarried of it already.

VAINLOVE

Well, good-morrow. Let's dine together; I'll meet at the old place.

BELLMOUR

With all my heart. It lies convenient for us to pay our afternoon services to our mistresses. I find I am damnably in love, I'm so uneasy for not having seen Belinda yesterday.

VAINLOVE

But I saw my Araminta, yet am as impatient.

SCENE II

BELLMOUR alone.

BELLMOUR

Why, what a cormorant in love am I! Who, not contented with the slavery of honourable love in one place, and the pleasure of enjoying some half a score mistresses of my own acquiring, must yet take Vainlove's business upon my hands, because it lay too heavy upon his; so am not only forced to lie with other men's wives for 'em, but must also undertake the harder task of obliging their mistresses. I must take up, or I shall never hold out. Flesh and blood cannot bear it always.

SCENE III

[To him **SHARPER**.

SHARPER

I'm sorry to see this, Ned. Once a man comes to his soliloquies, I give him for gone.

BELLMOUR

Sharper, I'm glad to see thee.

SHARPER

What! is Belinda cruel, that you are so thoughtful?

BELLMOUR

No, faith, not for that. But there's a business of consequence fallen out to-day that requires some consideration.

SHARPER

Prithee, what mighty business of consequence canst thou have?

BELLMOUR

Why, you must know, 'tis a piece of work toward the finishing of an alderman. It seems I must put the last hand to it, and dub him cuckold, that he may be of equal dignity with the rest of his brethren: so I must beg Belinda's pardon.

SHARPER

Faith, e'en give her over for good and all; you can have no hopes of getting her for a mistress; and she is too proud, too inconstant, too affected and too witty, and too handsome for a wife.

BELLMOUR

But she can't have too much money. There's twelve thousand pound, Tom. 'Tis true she is excessively foppish and affected; but in my conscience I believe the baggage loves me: for she never speaks well of me herself, nor suffers anybody else to rail at me. Then, as I told you, there's twelve thousand pound. Hum! Why, faith, upon second thoughts, she does not appear to be so very affected neither.—Give her her due, I think the woman's a woman, and that's all. As such, I'm sure I shall like her; for the devil take me if I don't love all the sex.

SHARPER

And here comes one who swears as heartily he hates all the sex.

SCENE IV

[To them **HEARTWELL**.

BELLMOUR

Who? Heartwell? Ay, but he knows better things. How now, George, where hast thou been snarling odious truths, and entertaining company, like a physician, with discourse of their diseases and infirmities? What fine lady hast thou been putting out of conceit with herself, and persuading that the face she had been making all the morning was none of her own? For I know thou art as unmannerly and as unwelcome to a woman as a looking-glass after the smallpox.

HEARTWELL

I confess I have not been sneering fulsome lies and nauseous flattery; fawning upon a little tawdry whore, that will fawn upon me again, and entertain any puppy that comes, like a tumbler, with the same tricks over and over. For such, I guess, may have been your late employment.

BELLMOUR
Would thou hadst come a little sooner. Vainlove would have wrought thy conversion, and been a champion for the cause.

HEARTWELL
What! has he been here? That's one of love's April fools; is always upon some errand that's to no purpose; ever embarking in adventures, yet never comes to harbour.

SHARPER
That's because he always sets out in foul weather, loves to buffet with the winds, meet the tide, and sail in the teeth of opposition.

HEARTWELL
What! Has he not dropt anchor at Araminta?

BELLMOUR
Truth on't is she fits his temper best, is a kind of floating island; sometimes seems in reach, then vanishes and keeps him busied in the search.

SHARPER
She had need have a good share of sense to manage so capricious a lover.

BELLMOUR
Faith I don't know, he's of a temper the most easy to himself in the world; he takes as much always of an amour as he cares for, and quits it when it grows stale or unpleasant.

SHARPER
An argument of very little passion, very good understanding, and very ill nature.

HEARTWELL
And proves that Vainlove plays the fool with discretion.

SHARPER
You, Bellmour, are bound in gratitude to stickle for him; you with pleasure reap that fruit, which he takes pains to sow: he does the drudgery in the mine, and you stamp your image on the gold.

BELLMOUR
He's of another opinion, and says I do the drudgery in the mine. Well, we have each our share of sport, and each that which he likes best; 'tis his diversion to set, 'tis mine to cover the partridge.

HEARTWELL
And it should be mine to let 'em go again.

SHARPER

Not till you had mouthed a little, George. I think that's all thou art fit for now.

HEARTWELL
Good Mr. Young-Fellow, you're mistaken; as able as yourself, and as nimble, too, though I mayn't have so much mercury in my limbs; 'tis true, indeed, I don't force appetite, but wait the natural call of my lust, and think it time enough to be lewd after I have had the temptation.

BELLMOUR
Time enough, ay, too soon, I should rather have expected, from a person of your gravity.

HEARTWELL
Yet it is oftentimes too late with some of you young, termagant, flashy sinners—you have all the guilt of the intention, and none of the pleasure of the practice—'tis true you are so eager in pursuit of the temptation, that you save the devil the trouble of leading you into it. Nor is it out of discretion that you don't swallow that very hook yourselves have baited, but you are cloyed with the preparative, and what you mean for a whet, turns the edge of your puny stomachs. Your love is like your courage, which you show for the first year or two upon all occasions; till in a little time, being disabled or disarmed, you abate of your vigour; and that daring blade which was so often drawn, is bound to the peace for ever after.

BELLMOUR
Thou art an old fornicator of a singular good principle indeed, and art for encouraging youth, that they may be as wicked as thou art at thy years.

HEARTWELL
I am for having everybody be what they pretend to be: a whoremaster be a whoremaster, and not like Vainlove, kiss a lap-dog with passion, when it would disgust him from the lady's own lips.

BELLMOUR
That only happens sometimes, where the dog has the sweeter breath, for the more cleanly conveyance. But, George, you must not quarrel with little gallantries of this nature: women are often won by 'em. Who would refuse to kiss a lap-dog, if it were preliminary to the lips of his lady?

SHARPER
Or omit playing with her fan, and cooling her if she were hot, when it might entitle him to the office of warming her when she should be cold?

BELLMOUR
What is it to read a play in a rainy day? Though you should be now and then interrupted in a witty scene, and she perhaps preserve her laughter, till the jest were over; even that may be borne with, considering the reward in prospect.

HEARTWELL
I confess you that are women's asses bear greater burdens: are forced to undergo dressing, dancing, singing, sighing, whining, rhyming, flattering, lying, grinning, cringing, and the drudgery of loving to boot.

BELLMOUR
O brute, the drudgery of loving!

HEARTWELL

Ay! Why, to come to love through all these incumbrances is like coming to an estate overcharged with debts, which, by the time you have paid, yields no further profit than what the bare tillage and manuring of the land will produce at the expense of your own sweat.

BELLMOUR

Prithee, how dost thou love?

SHARPER

He! He hates the sex.

HEARTWELL

So I hate physic too—yet I may love to take it for my health.

BELLMOUR

Well come off, George, if at any time you should be taken straying.

SHARPER

He has need of such an excuse, considering the present state of his body.

HEARTWELL

How d'ye mean?

SHARPER

Why, if whoring be purging, as you call it, then, I may say, marriage is entering into a course of physic.

BELLMOUR

How, George! Does the wind blow there?

HEARTWELL

It will as soon blow north and by south—marry, quotha! I hope in heaven I have a greater portion of grace, and I think I have baited too many of those traps to be caught in one myself.

BELLMOUR

Who the devil would have thee? unless 'twere an oyster-woman to propagate young fry for Billingsgate—thy talent will never recommend thee to anything of better quality.

HEARTWELL

My talent is chiefly that of speaking truth, which I don't expect should ever recommend me to people of quality. I thank heaven I have very honestly purchased the hatred of all the great families in town.

SHARPER

And you in return of spleen hate them. But could you hope to be received into the alliance of a noble family—

HEARTWELL

No; I hope I shall never merit that affliction, to be punished with a wife of birth, be a stag of the first head and bear my horns aloft, like one of the supporters of my wife's coat. S'death I would not be a Cuckold to e'er an illustrious whore in England.

BELLMOUR
What, not to make your family, man and provide for your children?

SHARPER
For her children, you mean.

HEARTWELL
Ay, there you've nicked it. There's the devil upon devil. Oh, the pride and joy of heart 'twould be to me to have my son and heir resemble such a duke; to have a fleering coxcomb scoff and cry, 'Mr. your son's mighty like his Grace, has just his smile and air of's face.' Then replies another, 'Methinks he has more of the Marquess of such a place about his nose and eyes, though he has my Lord what-d'ye-call's mouth to a tittle.' Then I, to put it off as unconcerned, come chuck the infant under the chin, force a smile, and cry, 'Ay, the boy takes after his mother's relations,' when the devil and she knows 'tis a little compound of the whole body of nobility.

BELLMOUR & SHARPER
Ha, ha, ha!

BELLMOUR
Well, but, George, I have one question to ask you—

HEARTWELL
Pshaw, I have prattled away my time. I hope you are in no haste for an answer, for I shan't stay now.

[Looking on his watch.]

BELLMOUR
Nay, prithee, George—

HEARTWELL
No; besides my business, I see a fool coming this way. Adieu.

SCENE V

SHARPER, BELLMOUR.

BELLMOUR
What does he mean? Oh, 'tis Sir Joseph Wittoll with his friend; but I see he has turned the corner and goes another way.

SHARPER
What in the name of wonder is it?

BELLMOUR

Why, a fool.

SHARPER

'Tis a tawdry outside.

BELLMOUR

And a very beggarly lining—yet he may be worth your acquaintance; a little of thy chymistry, Tom, may extract gold from that dirt.

SHARPER

Say you so? 'Faith I am as poor as a chymist, and would be as industrious. But what was he that followed him? Is not he a dragon that watches those golden pippins?

BELLMOUR

Hang him, no, he a dragon! If he be, 'tis a very peaceful one. I can ensure his anger dormant; or should he seem to rouse, 'tis but well lashing him, and he will sleep like a top.

SHARPER

Ay, is he of that kidney?

BELLMOUR

Yet is adored by that bigot, Sir Joseph Wittoll, as the image of valour. He calls him his back, and indeed they are never asunder—yet, last night, I know not by what mischance, the knight was alone, and had fallen into the hands of some night-walkers, who, I suppose, would have pillaged him. But I chanced to come by and rescued him, though I believe he was heartily frightened; for as soon as ever he was loose, he ran away without staying to see who had helped him.

SHARPER

Is that bully of his in the army?

BELLMOUR

No; but is a pretender, and wears the habit of a soldier, which nowadays as often cloaks cowardice, as a black gown does atheism. You must know he has been abroad—went purely to run away from a campaign; enriched himself with the plunder of a few oaths, and here vents them against the general, who, slighting men of merit, and preferring only those of interest, has made him quit the service.

SHARPER

Wherein no doubt he magnifies his own performance.

BELLMOUR

Speaks miracles, is the drum to his own praise—the only implement of a soldier he resembles, like that, being full of blustering noise and emptiness—

SHARPER

And like that, of no use but to be beaten.

BELLMOUR
Right; but then the comparison breaks, for he will take a drubbing with as little noise as a pulpit cushion.

SHARPER
His name, and I have done?

BELLMOUR
Why, that, to pass it current too, he has gilded with a title: he is called Capt. Bluffe.

SHARPER
Well, I'll endeavour his acquaintance—you steer another course, are bound—

For love's island: I, for the golden coast.
May each succeed in what he wishes most.

ACT II

SCENE I

SIR JOSEPH WITTOLL, SHARPER following.

SHARPER
Sure that's he, and alone.

SIR JOSEPH WITTOLL
Um—Ay, this, this is the very damned place; the inhuman cannibals, the bloody-minded villains, would have butchered me last night. No doubt they would have flayed me alive, have sold my skin, and devoured, etc.

SHARPER
How's this!

SIR JOSEPH WITTOLL
An it hadn't been for a civil gentleman as came by and frighted 'em away—but, agad, I durst not stay to give him thanks.

SHARPER
This must be Bellmour he means. Ha! I have a thought—

SIR JOSEPH WITTOLL
Zooks, would the captain would come; the very remembrance makes me quake; agad, I shall never be reconciled to this place heartily.

SHARPER
'Tis but trying, and being where I am at worst, now luck!—cursed fortune! this must be the place, this damned unlucky place—

SIR JOSEPH WITTOLL

Agad, and so 'tis. Why, here has been more mischief done, I perceive.

SHARPER

No, 'tis gone, 'tis lost—ten thousand devils on that chance which drew me hither; ay, here, just here, this spot to me is hell; nothing to be found, but the despair of what I've lost.

[Looking about as in search.]

SIR JOSEPH WITTOLL

Poor gentleman! By the Lord Harry I'll stay no longer, for I have found too—

SHARPER

Ha! who's that has found? What have you found? Restore it quickly, or by—

SIR JOSEPH WITTOLL

Not I, sir, not I; as I've a soul to be saved, I have found nothing but what has been to my loss, as I may say, and as you were saying, sir.

SHARPER

Oh, your servant, sir; you are safe, then, it seems. 'Tis an ill wind that blows nobody good. Well, you may rejoice over my ill fortune, since it paid the price of your ransom.

SIR JOSEPH WITTOLL

I rejoice! agad, not I, sir: I'm very sorry for your loss, with all my heart, blood and guts, sir; and if you did but know me, you'd ne'er say I were so ill-natured.

SHARPER

Know you! Why, can you be so ungrateful to forget me?

SIR JOSEPH WITTOLL

O Lord, forget him! No, no, sir, I don't forget you—because I never saw your face before, agad. Ha, ha, ha!

SHARPER [Angrily]

How!

SIR JOSEPH WITTOLL

Stay, stay, sir, let me recollect—he's a damned angry fellow—I believe I had better remember him, until I can get out of his sight; but out of sight out of mind, agad. [Aside.]

SHARPER

Methought the service I did you last night, sir, in preserving you from those ruffians, might have taken better root in your shallow memory.

SIR JOSEPH WITTOLL

Gads-daggers-belts-blades and scabbards, this is the very gentleman! How shall I make him a return suitable to the greatness of his merit? I had a pretty thing to that purpose, if he ha'n't frighted it out of my memory. Hem! hem! sir, I most submissively implore your pardon for my transgression of ingratitude and omission; having my entire dependence, sir, upon the superfluity of your goodness, which, like an inundation, will, I hope, totally immerge the recollection of my error, and leave me floating, in your sight, upon the full-blown bladders of repentance—by the help of which, I shall once more hope to swim into your favour.

[Bows.]

SHARPER
So-h, oh, sir, I am easily pacified, the acknowledgment of a gentleman—

SIR JOSEPH WITTOLL
Acknowledgment! Sir, I am all over acknowledgment, and will not stick to show it in the greatest extremity by night or by day, in sickness or in health, winter or summer; all seasons and occasions shall testify the reality and gratitude of your superabundant humble servant, Sir Joseph Wittoll, knight. Hem! hem!

SHARPER
Sir Joseph Wittoll?

SIR JOSEPH WITTOLL
The same, sir, of Wittoll Hall in Comitatu Bucks.

SHARPER
Is it possible! Then I am happy to have obliged the mirror of knighthood and pink of courtesie in the age. Let me embrace you.

SIR JOSEPH WITTOLL
O Lord, sir!

SHARPER
My loss I esteem as a trifle repaid with interest, since it has purchased me the friendship and acquaintance of the person in the world whose character I admire.

SIR JOSEPH WITTOLL
You are only pleased to say so, sir. But, pray, if I may be so bold, what is that loss you mention?

SHARPER
Oh, term it no longer so, sir. In the scuffle last night I only dropt a bill of a hundred pound, which, I confess, I came half despairing to recover; but, thanks to my better fortune—

SIR JOSEPH WITTOLL
You have found it, sir, then, it seems; I profess I'm heartily glad—

SHARPER

Sir, your humble servant. I don't question but you are, that you have so cheap an opportunity of expressing your gratitude and generosity, since the paying so trivial a sum will wholly acquit you and doubly engage me.

SIR JOSEPH WITTOLL
What a dickens does he mean by a trivial sum? [Aside.] But ha'n't you found it, sir!

SHARPER
No otherwise, I vow to Gad, but in my hopes in you, sir.

SIR JOSEPH WITTOLL
Humh.

SHARPER
But that's sufficient. 'Twere injustice to doubt the honour of Sir Joseph Wittoll.

SIR JOSEPH WITTOLL
O Lord, sir.

SHARPER
You are above, I'm sure, a thought so low, to suffer me to lose what was ventured in your service; nay, 'twas in a manner paid down for your deliverance; 'twas so much lent you. And you scorn, I'll say that for you—

SIR JOSEPH WITTOLL
Nay, I'll say that for myself, with your leave, sir, I do scorn a dirty thing. But, agad, I'm a little out of pocket at present.

SHARPER
Pshaw, you can't want a hundred pound. Your word is sufficient anywhere. 'Tis but borrowing so much dirt. You have large acres, and can soon repay it. Money is but dirt, Sir Joseph—mere dirt.

SIR JOSEPH WITTOLL
But, I profess, 'tis a dirt I have washed my hands of at present; I have laid it all out upon my Back.

SHARPER
Are you so extravagant in clothes, Sir Joseph?

SIR JOSEPH WITTOLL
Ha, ha, ha, a very good jest, I profess, ha, ha, ha, a very good jest, and I did not know that I had said it, and that's a better jest than t'other. 'Tis a sign you and I ha'n't been long acquainted; you have lost a good jest for want of knowing me—I only mean a friend of mine whom I call my Back; he sticks as close to me, and follows me through all dangers—he is indeed back, breast, and head-piece, as it were, to me. Agad, he's a brave fellow. Pauh, I am quite another thing when I am with him: I don't fear the devil, bless us, almost if he be by. Ah! had he been with me last night—

SHARPER

If he had, sir, what then? he could have done no more, nor perhaps have suffered so much. Had he a hundred pound to lose? [Angrily.]

SIR JOSEPH WITTOLL

O Lord, sir, by no means, but I might have saved a hundred pound: I meant innocently, as I hope to be saved, sir, a damned hot fellow, only, as I was saying, I let him have all my ready money to redeem his great sword from limbo. But, sir, I have a letter of credit to Alderman Fondlewife, as far as two hundred pound, and this afternoon you shall see I am a person, such a one as you would wish to have met with—

SHARPER

That you are, I'll be sworn. [Aside.] Why, that's great and like yourself.

SCENE II

[To them **CAPTAIN BLUFFE**.

SIR JOSEPH WITTOLL

Oh, here a' comes—Ay, my Hector of Troy, welcome, my bully, my Back; agad, my heart has gone a pit pat for thee.

CAPTAIN BLUFFE

How now, my young knight? Not for fear, I hope; he that knows me must be a stranger to fear.

SIR JOSEPH WITTOLL

Nay, agad, I hate fear ever since I had like to have died of a fright. But—

CAPTAIN BLUFFE

But? Look you here, boy, here's your antidote, here's your Jesuits' powder for a shaking fit. But who hast thou got with thee? is he of mettle?

[Laying his hand upon his sword.]

SIR JOSEPH WITTOLL

Ay, bully, a devilish smart fellow: 'a will fight like a cock.

CAPTAIN BLUFFE

Say you so? Then I honour him. But has he been abroad? for every cock will fight upon his own dunghill.

SIR JOSEPH WITTOLL

I don't know, but I'll present you—

CAPTAIN BLUFFE

I'll recommend myself. Sir, I honour you; I understand you love fighting, I reverence a man that loves fighting. Sir, I kiss your hilts.

SHARPER

Sir, your servant, but you are misinformed, for, unless it be to serve my particular friend, as Sir Joseph here, my country, or my religion, or in some very justifiable cause, I'm not for it.

CAPTAIN BLUFFE
O Lord, I beg your pardon, sir, I find you are not of my palate: you can't relish a dish of fighting without sweet sauce. Now, I think fighting for fighting sake's sufficient cause; fighting to me's religion and the laws.

SIR JOSEPH WITTOLL
Ah, well said, my Hero; was not that great, sir? by the Lord Harry he says true; fighting is meat, drink, and cloth to him. But, Back, this gentleman is one of the best friends I have in the world, and saved my life last night—you know I told you.

CAPTAIN BLUFFE
Ay! Then I honour him again. Sir, may I crave your name?

SHARPER
Ay, sir, my name's Sharper.

SIR JOSEPH WITTOLL
Pray, Mr. Sharper, embrace my Back. Very well. By the Lord Harry, Mr. Sharper, he's as brave a fellow as Cannibal, are not you, Bully-Back?

SHARPER
Hannibal, I believe you mean, Sir Joseph.

CAPTAIN BLUFFE
Undoubtedly he did, sir; faith, Hannibal was a very pretty fellow—but, Sir Joseph, comparisons are odious—Hannibal was a very pretty fellow in those days, it must be granted—but alas, sir! were he alive now, he would be nothing, nothing in the earth.

SHARPER
How, sir! I make a doubt if there be at this day a greater general breathing.

CAPTAIN BLUFFE
Oh, excuse me, sir! Have you served abroad, sir?

SHARPER
Not I, really, sir.

CAPTAIN BLUFFE
Oh, I thought so. Why, then, you can know nothing, sir: I am afraid you scarce know the history of the late war in Flanders, with all its particulars.

SHARPER
Not I, sir, no more than public letters or gazettes tell us.

CAPTAIN BLUFFE

Gazette! Why there again now. Why, sir, there are not three words of truth the year round put into the Gazette. I'll tell you a strange thing now as to that. You must know, sir, I was resident in Flanders the last campaign, had a small post there, but no matter for that. Perhaps, sir, there was scarce anything of moment done but an humble servant of yours, that shall be nameless, was an eye-witness of. I won't say had the greatest share in't, though I might say that too, since I name nobody you know. Well, Mr. Sharper, would you think it? In all this time, as I hope for a truncheon, this rascally gazette-writer never so much as once mentioned me—not once, by the wars—took no more notice than as if Nol. Bluffe had not been in the land of the living.

SHARPER
Strange!

SIR JOSEPH WITTOLL
Yet, by the Lord Harry, 'tis true, Mr. Sharper, for I went every day to coffee-houses to read the gazette myself.

CAPTAIN BLUFFE
Ay, ay, no matter. You see, Mr. Sharper, after all I am content to retire; live a private person. Scipio and others have done it.

SHARPER [Aside]
Impudent rogue.

SIR JOSEPH WITTOLL
Ay, this damned modesty of yours. Agad, if he would put in for't he might be made general himself yet.

CAPTAIN BLUFFE
Oh, fie! no, Sir Joseph; you know I hate this.

SIR JOSEPH WITTOLL
Let me but tell Mr. Sharper a little, how you ate fire once out of the mouth of a cannon. Agad, he did; those impenetrable whiskers of his have confronted flames—

CAPTAIN BLUFFE
Death, what do you mean, Sir Joseph?

SIR JOSEPH WITTOLL
Look you now. I tell you he's so modest he'll own nothing.

CAPTAIN BLUFFE [Angrily.]
Pish, you have put me out, I have forgot what I was about. Pray hold your tongue, and give me leave.

SIR JOSEPH WITTOLL
I am dumb.

CAPTAIN BLUFFE
This sword I think I was telling you of, Mr. Sharper. This sword I'll maintain to be the best divine, anatomist, lawyer, or casuist in Europe; it shall decide a controversy or split a cause—

SIR JOSEPH WITTOLL

Nay, now I must speak; it will split a hair, by the Lord Harry, I have seen it.

CAPTAIN BLUFFE

Zounds, sir, it's a lie; you have not seen it, nor sha'n't see it; sir, I say you can't see; what d'ye say to that now?

SIR JOSEPH WITTOLL

I am blind.

CAPTAIN BLUFFE

Death, had any other man interrupted me—

SIR JOSEPH WITTOLL

Good Mr. Sharper, speak to him; I dare not look that way.

SHARPER

Captain, Sir Joseph's penitent.

CAPTAIN BLUFFE

Oh, I am calm, sir, calm as a discharged culverin. But 'twas indiscreet, when you know what will provoke me. Nay, come, Sir Joseph, you know my heat's soon over.

SIR JOSEPH WITTOLL

Well, I am a fool sometimes, but I'm sorry.

CAPTAIN BLUFFE

Enough.

SIR JOSEPH WITTOLL

Come, we'll go take a glass to drown animosities. Mr. Sharper, will you partake?

SHARPER

I wait on you, sir. Nay, pray, Captain; you are Sir Joseph's back.

SCENE III

ARAMINTA, BELINDA, BETTY waiting, in Araminta's apartment.

BELINDA

Ah! nay, dear; prithee, good, dear, sweet cousin, no more. O Gad! I swear you'd make one sick to hear you.

ARAMINTA

Bless me! what have I said to move you thus?

BELINDA

Oh, you have raved, talked idly, and all in commendation of that filthy, awkward, two-legged creature man. You don't know what you've said; your fever has transported you.

ARAMINTA

If love be the fever which you mean, kind heaven avert the cure. Let me have oil to feed that flame, and never let it be extinct till I myself am ashes.

BELINDA

There was a whine! O Gad, I hate your horrid fancy. This love is the devil, and, sure, to be in love is to be possessed. 'Tis in the head, the heart, the blood, the—all over. O Gad, you are quite spoiled. I shall loathe the sight of mankind for your sake.

ARAMINTA

Fie! this is gross affectation. A little of Bellmour's company would change the scene.

BELINDA

Filthy fellow! I wonder, cousin—

ARAMINTA

I wonder, cousin, you should imagine I don't perceive you love him.

BELINDA

Oh, I love your hideous fancy! Ha, ha, ha, love a man!

ARAMINTA

Love a man! yes, you would not love a beast.

BELINDA

Of all beasts not an ass—which is so like your Vainlove. Lard, I have seen an ass look so chagrin, ha, ha, ha, you must pardon me, I can't help laughing, that an absolute lover would have concluded the poor creature to have had darts, and flames, and altars, and all that in his breast. Araminta, come, I'll talk seriously to you now; could you but see with my eyes the buffoonery of one scene of address, a lover, set out with all his equipage and appurtenances; O Gad I sure you would—But you play the game, and consequently can't see the miscarriages obvious to every stander by.

ARAMINTA

Yes, yes; I can see something near it when you and Bellmour meet. You don't know that you dreamt of Bellmour last night, and called him aloud in your sleep.

BELINDA

Pish, I can't help dreaming of the devil sometimes; would you from thence infer I love him?

ARAMINTA

But that's not all; you caught me in your arms when you named him, and pressed me to your bosom. Sure, if I had not pinched you until you waked, you had stifled me with kisses.

BELINDA

O barbarous aspersion!

ARAMINTA

No aspersion, cousin, we are alone. Nay, I can tell you more.

BELINDA

I deny it all.

ARAMINTA

What, before you hear it?

BELINDA

My denial is premeditated like your malice. Lard, cousin, you talk oddly. Whatever the matter is, O my Sol, I'm afraid you'll follow evil courses.

ARAMINTA

Ha, ha, ha, this is pleasant.

BELINDA

You may laugh, but—

ARAMINTA

Ha, ha, ha!

BELINDA

You think the malicious grin becomes you. The devil take Bellmour. Why do you tell me of him?

ARAMINTA

Oh, is it come out? Now you are angry, I am sure you love him. I tell nobody else, cousin. I have not betrayed you yet.

BELINDA

Prithee tell it all the world; it's false.

ARAMINTA

Come, then, kiss and friends.

BELINDA

Pish.

ARAMINTA

Prithee don't be so peevish.

BELINDA

Prithee don't be so impertinent. Betty!

ARAMINTA

Ha, ha, ha!

BETTY
Did your ladyship call, madam?

BELINDA
Get my hoods and tippet, and bid the footman call a chair.

ARAMINTA
I hope you are not going out in dudgeon, cousin.

SCENE IV

[To them **FOOTMAN**.

FOOTMAN
Madam, there are—

BELINDA
Is there a chair?

FOOTMAN
No, madam, there are Mr. Bellmour and Mr. Vainlove to wait upon your ladyship.

ARAMINTA
Are they below?

FOOTMAN
No, madam, they sent before, to know if you were at home.

BELINDA
The visit's to you, cousin; I suppose I am at my liberty.

ARAMINTA
Be ready to show 'em up.

SCENE V

[To them **BETTY**, with Hoods and Looking-glass.

ARAMINTA
I can't tell, cousin; I believe we are equally concerned. But if you continue your humour, it won't be very entertaining. (I know she'd fain be persuaded to stay.) [Aside.]

BELINDA

I shall oblige you, in leaving you to the full and free enjoyment of that conversation you admire. Let me see; hold the glass. Lard, I look wretchedly to-day!

ARAMINTA

Betty, why don't you help my cousin?

[Putting on her hoods.]

BELINDA

Hold off your fists, and see that he gets a chair with a high roof, or a very low seat. Stay, come back here, you Mrs. Fidget—you are so ready to go to the footman. Here, take 'em all again, my mind's changed; I won't go.

SCENE VI

ARAMINTA, BELINDA.

ARAMINTA

So, this I expected. You won't oblige me, then, cousin, and let me have all the company to myself?

BELINDA

No; upon deliberation, I have too much charity to trust you to yourself. The devil watches all opportunities; and in this favourable disposition of your mind, heaven knows how far you may be tempted: I am tender of your reputation.

ARAMINTA

I am obliged to you. But who's malicious now, Belinda?

BELINDA

Not I; witness my heart, I stay out of pure affection.

ARAMINTA

In my conscience I believe you.

SCENE VII

[To them **VAINLOVE, BELLMOUR, FOOTMAN.**

BELLMOUR

So, fortune be praised! To find you both within, ladies, is—

ARAMINTA

No miracle, I hope.

BELLMOUR

Not o' your side, madam, I confess. But my tyrant there and I, are two buckets that can never come together.

BELINDA

Nor are ever like. Yet we often meet and clash.

BELLMOUR

How never like! marry, Hymen forbid. But this it is to run so extravagantly in debt; I have laid out such a world of love in your service, that you think you can never be able to pay me all. So shun me for the same reason that you would a dun.

BELINDA

Ay, on my conscience, and the most impertinent and troublesome of duns—a dun for money will be quiet, when he sees his debtor has not wherewithal. But a dun for love is an eternal torment that never rests—

BELLMOUR

Until he has created love where there was none, and then gets it for his pains. For importunity in love, like importunity at Court, first creates its own interest and then pursues it for the favour.

ARAMINTA

Favours that are got by impudence and importunity, are like discoveries from the rack, when the afflicted person, for his ease, sometimes confesses secrets his heart knows nothing of.

VAINLOVE

I should rather think favours, so gained, to be due rewards to indefatigable devotion. For as love is a deity, he must be served by prayer.

BELINDA

O Gad, would you would all pray to love, then, and let us alone.

VAINLOVE

You are the temples of love, and 'tis through you, our devotion must be conveyed.

ARAMINTA

Rather poor silly idols of your own making, which upon the least displeasure you forsake and set up new. Every man now changes his mistress and his religion as his humour varies, or his interest.

VAINLOVE

O madam—

ARAMINTA

Nay, come, I find we are growing serious, and then we are in great danger of being dull. If my music-master be not gone, I'll entertain you with a new song, which comes pretty near my own opinion of love and your sex. Who's there? Is Mr. Gavot gone? [Calls.]

FOOTMAN

Only to the next door, madam. I'll call him.

ARAMINTA, BELINDA, VAINLOVE, and **BELLMOUR.**

BELLMOUR

Why, you won't hear me with patience.

ARAMINTA

What's the matter, cousin?

BELLMOUR

Nothing, madam, only—

BELINDA

Prithee hold thy tongue. Lard, he has so pestered me with flames and stuff, I think I sha'n't endure the sight of a fire this twelvemonth.

BELLMOUR

Yet all can't melt that cruel frozen heart.

BELINDA

O Gad, I hate your hideous fancy—you said that once before—if you must talk impertinently, for Heaven's sake let it be with variety; don't come always, like the devil, wrapt in flames. I'll not hear a sentence more, that begins with an 'I burn'—or an 'I beseech you, madam.'

BELLMOUR

But tell me how you would be adored. I am very tractable.

BELINDA

Then know, I would be adored in silence.

BELLMOUR

Humph, I thought so, that you might have all the talk to yourself. You had better let me speak; for if my thoughts fly to any pitch, I shall make villainous signs.

BELINDA

What will you get by that; to make such signs as I won't understand?

BELLMOUR

Ay, but if I'm tongue-tied, I must have all my actions free to—quicken your apprehension—and I—gad let me tell you, my most prevailing argument is expressed in dumb show.

[To them **MUSIC-MASTER**.

ARAMINTA

Oh, I am glad we shall have a song to divert the discourse. Pray oblige us with the last new song.

SONG

I

Thus to a ripe, consenting maid,
Poor, old, repenting Delia said,
Would you long preserve your lover?
Would you still his goddess reign?
Never let him all discover,
Never let him much obtain.

II

Men will admire, adore and die,
While wishing at your feet they lie:
But admitting their embraces,
Wakes 'em from the golden dream;
Nothing's new besides our faces,
Every woman is the same.

ARAMINTA

So, how de'e like the song, gentlemen?

BELLMOUR

Oh, very well performed; but I don't much admire the words.

ARAMINTA

I expected it; there's too much truth in 'em. If Mr. Gavot will walk with us in the garden, we'll have it once again; you may like it better at second hearing. You'll bring my cousin.

BELLMOUR

Faith, madam, I dare not speak to her, but I'll make signs.

[Addresses **BELINDA** in dumb show.]

BELINDA

Oh, foh, your dumb rhetoric is more ridiculous than your talking impertinence, as an ape is a much more troublesome animal than a parrot.

ARAMINTA

Ay, cousin, and 'tis a sign the creatures mimic nature well; for there are few men but do more silly things than they say.

BELLMOUR

Well, I find my apishness has paid the ransom for my speech, and set it at liberty—though, I confess, I could be well enough pleased to drive on a love-bargain in that silent manner—'twould save a man a world of lying and swearing at the year's end. Besides, I have had a little experience, that brings to mind—

When wit and reason both have failed to move;
Kind looks and actions, from success, do prove,
Ev'n silence may be eloquent in love.

ACT III

SCENE I. The Street.

SILVIA and **LUCY**.

SILVIA

Will he not come, then?

LUCY

Yes, yes; come, I warrant him, if you will go in and be ready to receive him.

SILVIA

Why did you not tell me? Whom mean you?

LUCY

Whom you should mean, Heartwell.

SILVIA

Senseless creature, I meant my Vainlove.

LUCY

You may as soon hope to recover your own maiden-head as his love. Therefore, e'en set your heart at rest, and in the name of opportunity mind your own business. Strike Heartwell home before the bait's worn off the hook. Age will come. He nibbled fairly yesterday, and no doubt will be eager enough to-day to swallow the temptation.

SILVIA

Well, since there's no remedy—yet tell me—for I would know, though to the anguish of my soul, how did he refuse? Tell me, how did he receive my letter—in anger or in scorn?

LUCY

Neither; but what was ten times worse, with damned senseless indifference. By this light I could have spit in his face. Receive it! Why, he received it as I would one of your lovers that should come empty-handed; as a court lord does his mercer's bill or a begging dedication—he received it as if 't had been a letter from his wife.

SILVIA

What! did he not read it?

LUCY

Hummed it over, gave you his respects, and said he would take time to peruse it—but then he was in haste.

SILVIA

Respects, and peruse it! He's gone, and Araminta has bewitched him from me. Oh, how the name of rival fires my blood. I could curse 'em both; eternal jealousy attend her love, and disappointment meet his. Oh that I could revenge the torment he has caused; methinks I feel the woman strong within me, and vengeance kindles in the room of love.

LUCY

I have that in my head may make mischief.

SILVIA

How, dear Lucy?

LUCY

You know Araminta's dissembled coyness has won, and keeps him hers—

SILVIA

Could we persuade him that she loves another—

LUCY

No, you're out; could we persuade him that she dotes on him, himself. Contrive a kind letter as from her, 'twould disgust his nicety, and take away his stomach.

SILVIA

Impossible; 'twill never take.

LUCY

Trouble not your head. Let me alone—I will inform myself of what passed between 'em to-day, and about it straight. Hold, I'm mistaken, or that's Heartwell, who stands talking at the corner—'tis he—go get you in, madam, receive him pleasantly, dress up your face in innocence and smiles, and dissemble the very want of dissimulation. You know what will take him.

SILVIA

'Tis as hard to counterfeit love as it is to conceal it: but I'll do my weak endeavour, though I fear I have not art.

LUCY

Hang art, madam, and trust to nature for dissembling.

Man was by nature woman's cully made: We never are but by ourselves betrayed.

HEARTWELL, VAINLOVE and **BELLMOUR** following.

BELLMOUR
Hist, hist, is not that Heartwell going to Silvia?

VAINLOVE
He's talking to himself, I think; prithee let's try if we can hear him.

HEARTWELL
Why, whither in the devil's name am I agoing now? Hum—let me think—is not this Silvia's house, the cave of that enchantress, and which consequently I ought to shun as I would infection? To enter here is to put on the envenomed shirt, to run into the embraces of a fever, and in some raving fit, be led to plunge myself into that more consuming fire, a woman's arms. Ha! well recollected, I will recover my reason, and be gone.

BELLMOUR
Now Venus forbid!

VAINLOVE
Hush—

HEARTWELL
Well, why do you not move? Feet, do your office—not one inch; no, fore Gad I'm caught. There stands my north, and thither my needle points. Now could I curse myself, yet cannot repent. O thou delicious, damned, dear, destructive woman! S'death, how the young fellows will hoot me! I shall be the jest of the town: nay, in two days I expect to be chronicled in ditty, and sung in woful ballad, to the tune of the Superannuated Maiden's Comfort, or the Bachelor's Fall; and upon the third, I shall be hanged in effigy, pasted up for the exemplary ornament of necessary houses and cobblers' stalls. Death, I can't think on't—I'll run into the danger to lose the apprehension.

BELLMOUR, VAINLOVE.

BELLMOUR
A very certain remedy, probatum est. Ha, ha, ha, poor George, thou art i' th' right, thou hast sold thyself to laughter; the ill-natured town will find the jest just where thou hast lost it. Ha, ha, how a' struggled, like an old lawyer between two fees.

VAINLOVE
Or a young wench between pleasure and reputation.

BELLMOUR

Or as you did to-day, when half afraid you snatched a kiss from Araminta.

VAINLOVE

She has made a quarrel on't.

BELLMOUR

Pauh, women are only angry at such offences to have the pleasure of forgiving them.

VAINLOVE

And I love to have the pleasure of making my peace. I should not esteem a pardon if too easily won.

BELLMOUR

Thou dost not know what thou wouldst be at; whether thou wouldst have her angry or pleased. Couldst thou be content to marry Araminta?

VAINLOVE

Could you be content to go to heaven?

BELLMOUR

Hum, not immediately, in my conscience not heartily. I'd do a little more good in my generation first, in order to deserve it.

VAINLOVE

Nor I to marry Araminta till I merit her.

BELLMOUR

But how the devil dost thou expect to get her if she never yield?

VAINLOVE

That's true; but I would—

BELLMOUR

Marry her without her consent; thou 'rt a riddle beyond woman—

SCENE IV

[To them **SETTER**.

Trusty Setter, what tidings? How goes the project?

SETTER

As all lewd projects do, sir, where the devil prevents our endeavours with success.

BELLMOUR

A good hearing, Setter.

VAINLOVE
Well, I'll leave you with your engineer.

BELLMOUR
And hast thou provided necessaries?

SETTER
All, all, sir; the large sanctified hat, and the little precise band, with a swinging long spiritual cloak, to cover carnal knavery—not forgetting the black patch, which Tribulation Spintext wears, as I'm informed, upon one eye, as a penal mourning for the ogling offences of his youth; and some say, with that eye he first discovered the frailty of his wife.

BELLMOUR
Well, in this fanatic father's habit will I confess Lætitia.

SETTER
Rather prepare her for confession, sir, by helping her to sin.

BELLMOUR
Be at your master's lodging in the evening; I shall use the robes.

SCENE V

SETTER alone.

SETTER
I shall, sir. I wonder to which of these two gentlemen I do most properly appertain: the one uses me as his attendant; the other, being the better acquainted with my parts, employs me as a pimp; why, that's much the more honourable employment—by all means. I follow one as my master, the other follows me as his conductor.

SCENE VI

[To him **LUCY**.

LUCY
There's the hang-dog, his man—I had a power over him in the reign of my mistress; but he is too true a Valet de Chambre not to affect his master's faults, and consequently is revolted from his allegiance.

SETTER
Undoubtedly 'tis impossible to be a pimp and not a man of parts. That is without being politic, diligent, secret, wary, and so forth—and to all this valiant as Hercules—that is, passively valiant and actively obedient. Ah, Setter, what a treasure is here lost for want of being known.

LUCY

Here's some villainy afoot; he's so thoughtful. May be I may discover something in my mask. Worthy sir, a word with you.

[Puts on her mask.]

SETTER

Why, if I were known, I might come to be a great man—

LUCY

Not to interrupt your meditation—

SETTER

And I should not be the first that has procured his greatness by pimping.

LUCY

Now poverty and the pox light upon thee for a contemplative pimp.

SETTER

Ha! what art who thus maliciously hast awakened me from my dream of glory? Speak, thou vile disturber—

LUCY

Of thy most vile cogitations—thou poor, conceited wretch, how wert thou valuing thyself upon thy master's employment? For he's the head pimp to Mr. Bellmour.

SETTER

Good words, damsel, or I shall—But how dost thou know my master or me?

LUCY

Yes; I know both master and man to be—

SETTER

To be men, perhaps; nay, faith, like enough: I often march in the rear of my master, and enter the breaches which he has made.

LUCY

Ay, the breach of faith, which he has begun: thou traitor to thy lawful princess.

SETTER

Why, how now! prithee who art? Lay by that worldly face and produce your natural vizor.

LUCY

No, sirrah, I'll keep it on to abuse thee and leave thee without hopes of revenge.

SETTER

Oh! I begin to smoke ye: thou art some forsaken Abigail we have dallied with heretofore—and art come to tickle thy imagination with remembrance of iniquity past.

LUCY
No thou pitiful flatterer of thy master's imperfections; thou maukin made up of the shreds and parings of his superfluous fopperies.

SETTER
Thou art thy mistress's foul self, composed of her sullied iniquities and clothing.

LUCY
Hang thee, beggar's cur, thy master is but a mumper in love, lies canting at the gate; but never dares presume to enter the house.

SETTER
Thou art the wicket to thy mistress's gate, to be opened for all comers. In fine thou art the highroad to thy mistress.

LUCY
Beast, filthy toad, I can hold no longer, look and tremble.

[Unmasks.]

SETTER
How, Mrs. Lucy!

LUCY
I wonder thou hast the impudence to look me in the face.

SETTER
Adsbud, who's in fault, mistress of mine? who flung the first stone? who undervalued my function? and who the devil could know you by instinct?

LUCY
You could know my office by instinct, and be hanged, which you have slandered most abominably. It vexes me not what you said of my person; but that my innocent calling should be exposed and scandalised—I cannot bear it.

SETTER
Nay, faith, Lucy, I'm sorry, I'll own myself to blame, though we were both in fault as to our offices— come, I'll make you any reparation.

LUCY
Swear.

SETTER
I do swear to the utmost of my power.

LUCY
To be brief, then; what is the reason your master did not appear to-day according to the summons I brought him?

SETTER
To answer you as briefly—he has a cause to be tried in another court.

LUCY
Come, tell me in plain terms, how forward he is with Araminta.

SETTER
Too forward to be turned back—though he's a little in disgrace at present about a kiss which he forced. You and I can kiss, Lucy, without all that.

LUCY
Stand off—he's a precious jewel.

SETTER
And therefore you'd have him to set in your lady's locket.

LUCY
Where is he now?

SETTER
He'll be in the Piazza presently.

LUCY
Remember to-day's behaviour. Let me see you with a penitent face.

SETTER
What, no token of amity, Lucy? You and I don't use to part with dry lips.

LUCY
No, no, avaunt—I'll not be slabbered and kissed now—I'm not i' th' humour.

SETTER
I'll not quit you so. I'll follow and put you into the humour.

SCENE VII

SIR JOSEPH WITTOLL, BLUFFE.

CAPTAIN BLUFFE
And so, out of your unwonted generosity—

SIR JOSEPH WITTOLL

And good-nature, Back; I am good-natured and I can't help it.

CAPTAIN BLUFFE
You have given him a note upon Fondlewife for a hundred pound.

SIR JOSEPH WITTOLL
Ay, ay, poor fellow; he ventured fair for't.

CAPTAIN BLUFFE
You have disobliged me in it—for I have occasion for the money, and if you would look me in the face again and live, go, and force him to redeliver you the note. Go, and bring it me hither. I'll stay here for you.

SIR JOSEPH WITTOLL
You may stay until the day of judgment, then, by the Lord Harry. I know better things than to be run through the guts for a hundred pounds. Why, I gave that hundred pound for being saved, and de'e think, an there were no danger, I'll be so ungrateful to take it from the gentleman again?

CAPTAIN BLUFFE
Well, go to him from me—tell him, I say, he must refund—or Bilbo's the world, and slaughter will ensue. If he refuse, tell him—but whisper that—tell him—I'll pink his soul. But whisper that softly to him.

SIR JOSEPH WITTOLL
So softly that he shall never hear on't, I warrant you. Why, what a devil's the matter, Bully; are you mad? or de'e think I'm mad? Agad, for my part, I don't love to be the messenger of ill news; 'tis an ungrateful office—so tell him yourself.

CAPTAIN BLUFFE
By these hilts I believe he frightened you into this composition: I believe you gave it him out of fear, pure, paltry fear—confess.

SIR JOSEPH WITTOLL
No, no, hang't; I was not afraid neither—though I confess he did in a manner snap me up—yet I can't say that it was altogether out of fear, but partly to prevent mischief—for he was a devilish choleric fellow. And if my choler had been up too, agad, there would have been mischief done, that's flat. And yet I believe if you had been by, I would as soon have let him a' had a hundred of my teeth. Adsheart, if he should come just now when I'm angry, I'd tell him—Mum.

SCENE VIII

[To them **BELLMOUR, SHARPER.**

BELLMOUR
Thou 'rt a lucky rogue; there's your benefactor; you ought to return him thanks now you have received the favour.

SHARPER

Sir Joseph! Your note was accepted, and the money paid at sight. I'm come to return my thanks—

SIR JOSEPH WITTOLL

They won't be accepted so readily as the bill, sir.

BELLMOUR

I doubt the knight repents, Tom. He looks like the knight of the sorrowful face.

SHARPER

This is a double generosity: do me a kindness and refuse my thanks. But I hope you are not offended that I offered them.

SIR JOSEPH WITTOLL

May be I am, sir, may be I am not, sir, may be I am both, sir; what then? I hope I may be offended without any offence to you, sir.

SHARPER

Hey day! Captain, what's the matter? You can tell.

CAPTAIN BLUFFE

Mr. Sharper, the matter is plain: Sir Joseph has found out your trick, and does not care to be put upon, being a man of honour.

SHARPER

Trick, sir?

SIR JOSEPH WITTOLL

Ay, trick, sir, and won't be put upon, sir, being a man of honour, sir, and so, sir—

SHARPER

Harkee, Sir Joseph, a word with ye. In consideration of some favours lately received, I would not have you draw yourself into a premunire, by trusting to that sign of a man there—that pot-gun charged with wind.

SIR JOSEPH WITTOLL

O Lord, O Lord, Captain, come justify yourself—I'll give him the lie if you'll stand to it.

SHARPER

Nay, then, I'll be beforehand with you, take that, oaf.

[Cuffs him.]

SIR JOSEPH WITTOLL

Captain, will you see this? Won't you pink his soul?

CAPTAIN BLUFFE

Husht, 'tis not so convenient now—I shall find a time.

SHARPER

What do you mutter about a time, rascal? You were the incendiary. There's to put you in mind of your time.—A memorandum.

[Kicks him.]

CAPTAIN BLUFFE

Oh, this is your time, sir; you had best make use on't.

SHARPER

I—Gad and so I will: there's again for you.

[Kicks him.]

CAPTAIN BLUFFE

You are obliging, sir, but this is too public a place to thank you in. But in your ear, you are to be seen again?

SHARPER

Ay, thou inimitable coward, and to be felt—as for example.

[Kicks him.]

BELLMOUR

Ha, ha, ha, prithee come away; 'tis scandalous to kick this puppy unless a man were cold and had no other way to get himself aheat.

SIR JOSEPH WITTOLL, CAPTAIN BLUFFE.

CAPTAIN BLUFFE

Very well—very fine—but 'tis no matter. Is not this fine, Sir Joseph?

SIR JOSEPH WITTOLL

Indifferent, agad, in my opinion, very indifferent. I'd rather go plain all my life than wear such finery.

CAPTAIN BLUFFE

Death and hell to be affronted thus! I'll die before I'll suffer it.

[Draws.]

SIR JOSEPH WITTOLL

O Lord, his anger was not raised before. Nay, dear Captain, don't be in passion now he's gone. Put up, put up, dear Back, 'tis your Sir Joseph begs, come let me kiss thee; so, so, put up, put up.

CAPTAIN BLUFFE
By heaven, 'tis not to be put up.

SIR JOSEPH WITTOLL
What, Bully?

CAPTAIN BLUFFE
The affront.

SIR JOSEPH WITTOLL
No, aged, no more 'tis, for that's put up all already; thy sword, I mean.

CAPTAIN BLUFFE
Well, Sir Joseph, at your entreaty—But were not you, my friend, abused, and cuffed, and kicked?

[Putting up his sword.]

SIR JOSEPH WITTOLL
Ay, ay, so were you too; no matter, 'tis past.

CAPTAIN BLUFFE
By the immortal thunder of great guns, 'tis false—he sucks not vital air who dares affirm it to this face.

[Looks big.]

SIR JOSEPH WITTOLL
To that face I grant you, Captain. No, no, I grant you—not to that face, by the Lord Harry. If you had put on your fighting face before, you had done his business—he durst as soon have kissed you, as kicked you to your face. But a man can no more help what's done behind his back than what's said—Come, we'll think no more of what's past.

CAPTAIN BLUFFE
I'll call a council of war within to consider of my revenge to come.

SCENE X

HEARTWELL, SILVIA. Silvia's apartment.

SONG
As Amoret and Thyrsis lay
Melting the hours in gentle play,
Joining faces, mingling kisses,
And exchanging harmless blisses:
He trembling cried, with eager haste,
O let me feed as well as taste,

I die, if I'm not wholly blest.

[After the song a dance of antics.]

SILVIA
Indeed it is very fine. I could look upon 'em all day.

HEARTWELL
Well has this prevailed for me, and will you look upon me?

SILVIA
If you could sing and dance so, I should love to look upon you too.

HEARTWELL
Why, 'twas I sung and danced; I gave music to the voice, and life to their measures. Look you here, Silvia,—

[Pulling out a purse and chinking it]

—here are songs and dances, poetry and music—hark! how sweetly one guinea rhymes to another—and how they dance to the music of their own chink. This buys all t'other—and this thou shalt have; this, and all that I am worth, for the purchase of thy love. Say, is it mine then, ha? Speak, Syren—Oons, why do I look on her! Yet I must. Speak, dear angel, devil, saint, witch; do not rack me with suspense.

SILVIA
Nay, don't stare at me so. You make me blush—I cannot look.

HEARTWELL
O manhood, where art thou? What am I come to? A woman's toy, at these years! Death, a bearded baby for a girl to dandle. O dotage, dotage! That ever that noble passion, lust, should ebb to this degree. No reflux of vigorous blood: but milky love supplies the empty channels; and prompts me to the softness of a child—a mere infant and would suck. Can you love me, Silvia? Speak.

SILVIA
I dare not speak until I believe you, and indeed I'm afraid to believe you yet.

HEARTWELL
Death, how her innocence torments and pleases me! Lying, child, is indeed the art of love, and men are generally masters in it: but I'm so newly entered, you cannot distrust me of any skill in the treacherous mystery. Now, by my soul, I cannot lie, though it were to serve a friend or gain a mistress.

SILVIA
Must you lie, then, if you say you love me?

HEARTWELL
No, no, dear ignorance, thou beauteous changeling—I tell thee I do love thee, and tell it for a truth, a naked truth, which I'm ashamed to discover.

SILVIA

But love, they say, is a tender thing, that will smooth frowns, and make calm an angry face; will soften a rugged temper, and make ill-humoured people good. You look ready to fright one, and talk as if your passion were not love, but anger.

HEARTWELL

'Tis both; for I am angry with myself when I am pleased with you. And a pox upon me for loving thee so well—yet I must on. 'Tis a bearded arrow, and will more easily be thrust forward than drawn back.

SILVIA

Indeed, if I were well assured you loved; but how can I be well assured?

HEARTWELL

Take the symptoms—and ask all the tyrants of thy sex if their fools are not known by this party-coloured livery. I am melancholic when thou art absent; look like an ass when thou art present; wake for thee when I should sleep; and even dream of thee when I am awake; sigh much, drink little, eat less, court solitude, am grown very entertaining to myself, and, as I am informed, very troublesome to everybody else. If this be not love, it is madness, and then it is pardonable. Nay, yet a more certain sign than all this, I give thee my money.

SILVIA

Ay, but that is no sign; for they say, gentlemen will give money to any naughty woman to come to bed to them. O Gemini, I hope you don't mean so—for I won't be a whore.

HEARTWELL [Aside.]

The more is the pity.

SILVIA

Nay, if you would marry me, you should not come to bed to me—you have such a beard, and would so prickle one. But do you intend to marry me?

HEARTWELL

That a fool should ask such a malicious question! Death, I shall be drawn in before I know where I am. However, I find I am pretty sure of her consent, if I am put to it. [Aside.] Marry you? No, no, I'll love you.

SILVIA

Nay, but if you love me, you must marry me. What, don't I know my father loved my mother and was married to her?

HEARTWELL

Ay, ay, in old days people married where they loved; but that fashion is changed, child.

SILVIA

Never tell me that; I know it is not changed by myself: for I love you, and would marry you.

HEARTWELL

I'll have my beard shaved, it sha'n't hurt thee, and we'll go to bed—

SILVIA

No, no, I'm not such a fool neither, but I can keep myself honest. Here, I won't keep anything that's yours; I hate you now,—

[Throws the purse]

—and I'll never see you again, 'cause you'd have me be naught.

[Going.]

HEARTWELL

Damn her, let her go, and a good riddance. Yet so much tenderness and beauty and honesty together is a jewel. Stay, Silvia—But then to marry; why, every man plays the fool once in his life. But to marry is playing the fool all one's life long.

SILVIA

What did you call me for?

HEARTWELL

I'll give thee all I have, and thou shalt live with me in everything so like my wife, the world shall believe it. Nay, thou shalt think so thyself—only let me not think so.

SILVIA

No, I'll die before I'll be your whore—as well as I love you.

HEARTWELL [Aside.]

A woman, and ignorant, may be honest, when 'tis out of obstinacy and contradiction. But, s'death, it is but a may be, and upon scurvy terms. Well, farewell then—if I can get out of sight I may get the better of myself.

SILVIA

Well—good-bye.

[Turns and weeps.]

HEARTWELL

Ha! Nay, come, we'll kiss at parting.

[Kisses her.]

By heaven, her kiss is sweeter than liberty. I will marry thee. There, thou hast done't. All my resolves melted in that kiss—one more.

SILVIA

But when?

HEARTWELL

I'm impatient until it be done; I will not give myself liberty to think, lest I should cool. I will about a licence straight—in the evening expect me. One kiss more to confirm me mad; so.

SILVIA
Ha, ha, ha, an old fox trapped—

SCENE XI

[To her **LUCY**.

Bless me! you frighted me; I thought he had been come again, and had heard me.

LUCY
Lord, madam, I met your lover in as much haste as if he had been going for a midwife.

SILVIA
He's going for a parson, girl, the forerunner of a midwife, some nine months hence. Well, I find dissembling to our sex is as natural as swimming to a negro; we may depend upon our skill to save us at a plunge, though till then, we never make the experiment. But how hast thou succeeded?

LUCY
As you would wish—since there is no reclaiming Vainlove. I have found out a pique she has taken at him, and have framed a letter that makes her sue for reconciliation first. I know that will do—walk in and I'll show it you. Come, madam, you're like to have a happy time on't; both your love and anger satisfied! All that can charm our sex conspire to please you.

That woman sure enjoys a blessed night, Whom love and vengeance both at once delight.

ACT IV

SCENE I. The Street

BELLMOUR, in fanatic habit, **SETTER**.

BELLMOUR
'Tis pretty near the hour.

[Looking on his watch.]

Well, and how, Setter, hae, does my hypocrisy fit me, hae? Does it sit easy on me?

SETTER
Oh, most religiously well, sir.

BELLMOUR

I wonder why all our young fellows should glory in an opinion of atheism, when they may be so much more conveniently lewd under the coverlet of religion.

SETTER

S'bud, sir, away quickly: there's Fondlewife just turned the corner, and 's coming this way.

BELLMOUR

Gad's so, there he is: he must not see me.

SCENE II

FONDLEWIFE, BARNABY.

FONDLEWIFE

I say I will tarry at home.

BARNABY

But, sir.

FONDLEWIFE

Good lack! I profess the spirit of contradiction hath possessed the lad—I say I will tarry at home, varlet.

BARNABY

I have done, sir; then farewell five hundred pound.

FONDLEWIFE

Ha, how's that? Stay, stay, did you leave word, say you, with his wife? With Comfort herself?

BARNABY

I did; and Comfort will send Tribulation hither as soon as ever he comes home. I could have brought young Mr. Prig to have kept my mistress company in the meantime. But you say—

FONDLEWIFE

How, how, say, varlet! I say let him not come near my doors. I say, he is a wanton young Levite, and pampereth himself up with dainties, that he may look lovely in the eyes of women. Sincerely, I am afraid he hath already defiled the tabernacle of our sister Comfort; while her good husband is deluded by his godly appearance. I say that even lust doth sparkle in his eyes and glow upon his cheeks, and that I would as soon trust my wife with a lord's high-fed chaplain.

BARNABY

Sir, the hour draws nigh, and nothing will be done here until you come.

FONDLEWIFE

And nothing can be done here until I go; so that I'll tarry, de'e see.

BARNABY

And run the hazard to lose your affair, sir!

FONDLEWIFE

Good lack, good lack—I profess it is a very sufficient vexation for a man to have a handsome wife.

BARNABY

Never, sir, but when the man is an insufficient husband. 'Tis then, indeed, like the vanity of taking a fine house, and yet be forced to let lodgings to help pay the rent.

FONDLEWIFE

I profess a very apt comparison, varlet. Go and bid my Cocky come out to me; I will give her some instructions, I will reason with her before I go.

SCENE III

FONDLEWIFE alone.

And in the meantime I will reason with myself. Tell me, Isaac, why art thee jealous? Why art thee distrustful of the wife of thy bosom? Because she is young and vigorous, and I am old and impotent. Then why didst thee marry, Isaac? Because she was beautiful and tempting, and because I was obstinate and doting; so that my inclination was, and is still, greater than my power. And will not that which tempted thee, also tempt others, who will tempt her, Isaac? I fear it much. But does not thy wife love thee, nay, dote upon thee? Yes. Why then! Ay, but to say truth, she's fonder of me than she has reason to be; and in the way of trade, we still suspect the smoothest dealers of the deepest designs. And that she has some designs deeper than thou canst reach, thou hast experimented, Isaac. But, mum.

SCENE IV

FONDLEWIFE, LÆTITIA.

LÆTITIA

I hope my dearest jewel is not going to leave me—are you, Nykin?

FONDLEWIFE

Wife—have you thoroughly considered how detestable, how heinous, and how crying a sin the sin of adultery is? Have you weighed it, I say? For it is a very weighty sin; and although it may lie heavy upon thee, yet thy husband must also bear his part. For thy iniquity will fall upon his head.

LÆTITIA

Bless me, what means my dear?

FONDLEWIFE

[Aside.] I profess she has an alluring eye; I am doubtful whether I shall trust her, even with Tribulation himself. Speak, I say, have you considered what it is to cuckold your husband?

LÆTITIA
[Aside.] I'm amazed. Sure he has discovered nothing. Who has wronged me to my dearest? I hope my jewel does not think that ever I had any such thing in my head, or ever will have.

FONDLEWIFE
No, no, I tell you I shall have it in my head—

LÆTITIA [Aside.]
I know not what to think. But I'm resolved to find the meaning of it. Unkind dear! Was it for this you sent to call me? Is it not affliction enough that you are to leave me, but you must study to increase it by unjust suspicions?

[Crying.]

Well—well—you know my fondness, and you love to tyrannise—Go on, cruel man, do: triumph over my poor heart while it holds, which cannot be long, with this usage of yours. But that's what you want. Well, you will have your ends soon. You will—you will. Yes, it will break to oblige you.

[Sighs.]

FONDLEWIFE
Verily, I fear I have carried the jest too far. Nay, look you now if she does not weep—'tis the fondest fool. Nay, Cocky, Cocky, nay, dear Cocky, don't cry, I was but in jest, I was not, ifeck.

LÆTITIA [Aside.]
Oh then, all's safe. I was terribly frighted. My affliction is always your jest, barbarous man! Oh, that I should love to this degree! Yet—

FONDLEWIFE
Nay, Cocky.

LÆTITIA
No, no, you are weary of me, that's it—that's all, you would get another wife—another fond fool, to break her heart—Well, be as cruel as you can to me, I'll pray for you; and when I am dead with grief, may you have one that will love you as well as I have done: I shall be contented to lie at peace in my cold grave—since it will please you.

[Sighs.]

FONDLEWIFE
Good lack, good lack, she would melt a heart of oak—I profess I can hold no longer. Nay, dear Cocky— ifeck, you'll break my heart—ifeck you will. See, you have made me weep—made poor Nykin weep. Nay, come kiss, buss poor Nykin—and I won't leave thee—I'll lose all first.

LÆTITIA [Aside.]

How! Heaven forbid! that will be carrying the jest too far indeed.

FONDLEWIFE
Won't you kiss Nykin?

LÆTITIA
Go, naughty Nykin, you don't love me.

FONDLEWIFE
Kiss, kiss, ifeck, I do.

LÆTITIA
No, you don't.

[She kisses him.]

FONDLEWIFE
What, not love Cocky!

LÆTITIA
No-h.

[Sighs.]

FONDLEWIFE
I profess I do love thee better than five hundred pound—and so thou shalt say, for I'll leave it to stay with thee.

LÆTITIA
No you sha'n't neglect your business for me. No, indeed, you sha'n't, Nykin. If you don't go, I'll think you been dealous of me still.

FONDLEWIFE
He, he, he, wilt thou, poor fool? Then I will go, I won't be dealous. Poor Cocky, kiss Nykin, kiss Nykin, ee, ee, ee. Here will be the good man anon, to talk to Cocky and teach her how a wife ought to behave herself.

LÆTITIA [Aside.]
I hope to have one that will show me how a husband ought to behave himself. I shall be glad to learn, to please my jewel.

[Kiss.]

FONDLEWIFE
That's my good dear. Come, kiss Nykin once more, and then get you in. So—get you in, get you in. Bye, bye.

LÆTITIA

Bye, Nykin.

FONDLEWIFE
Bye, Cocky.

LÆTITIA
Bye, Nykin.

FONDLEWIFE
Bye, Cocky, bye, bye.

SCENE V

VAINLOVE, SHARPER.

SHARPER
How! Araminta lost!

VAINLOVE
To confirm what I have said, read this.

[Gives a letter.]

SHARPER [Reads.]
Hum, hum! And what then appeared a fault, upon reflection seems only an effect of a too powerful passion. I'm afraid I give too great a proof of my own at this time. I am in disorder for what I have written. But something, I know not what, forced me. I only beg a favourable censure of this and your ARAMINTA.

SHARPER
Lost! Pray heaven thou hast not lost thy wits. Here, here, she's thy own, man, signed and sealed too. To her, man—a delicious melon, pure and consenting ripe, and only waits thy cutting up: she has been breeding love to thee all this while, and just now she's delivered of it.

VAINLOVE
'Tis an untimely fruit, and she has miscarried of her love.

SHARPER
Never leave this damned ill-natured whimsey, Frank? Thou hast a sickly, peevish appetite; only chew love and cannot digest it.

VAINLOVE
Yes, when I feed myself. But I hate to be crammed. By heaven, there's not a woman will give a man the pleasure of a chase: my sport is always balked or cut short. I stumble over the game I would pursue. 'Tis dull and unnatural to have a hare run full in the hounds' mouth, and would distaste the keenest hunter. I would have overtaken, not have met, my game.

SHARPER
However, I hope you don't mean to forsake it; that will be but a kind of mongrel cur's trick. Well, are you for the Mall?

VAINLOVE
No; she will be there this evening. Yes, I will go too, and she shall see her error in—

SHARPER
In her choice, I-gad. But thou canst not be so great a brute as to slight her.

VAINLOVE
I should disappoint her if I did not. By her management I should think she expects it.

All naturally fly what does pursue: 'Tis fit men should be coy when women woo.

SCENE VI

A Room in Fondlewife's House.

A **SERVANT** introducing **BELLMOUR**, in fanatic habit, with a patch upon one eye and a book in his hand.

SERVANT
Here's a chair, sir, if you please to repose yourself. My mistress is coming, sir.

BELLMOUR
Secure in my disguise I have out-faced suspicion and even dared discovery. This cloak my sanctity, and trusty Scarron's novels my prayer-book; methinks I am the very picture of Montufar in the Hypocrites. Oh! she comes.

SCENE VII

BELLMOUR, LÆTITIA.

So breaks Aurora through the veil of night, Thus fly the clouds, divided by her light, And every eye receives a new-born sight.

[Throwing off his cloak, patch, etc.]

LÆTITIA
Thus strewed with blushes, like—Ah! Heaven defend me! Who's this?

[Discovering him, starts.]

BELLMOUR

Your lover.

LÆTITIA [Aside.]

Vainlove's friend! I know his face, and he has betrayed me to him.

BELLMOUR

You are surprised. Did you not expect a lover, madam? Those eyes shone kindly on my first appearance, though now they are o'ercast.

LÆTITIA

I may well be surprised at your person and impudence: they are both new to me. You are not what your first appearance promised: the piety of your habit was welcome, but not the hypocrisy.

BELLMOUR

Rather the hypocrisy was welcome, but not the hypocrite.

LÆTITIA

Who are you, sir? You have mistaken the house sure.

BELLMOUR

I have directions in my pocket which agree with everything but your unkindness.

[Pulls out the letter.]

LÆTITIA

My letter! Base Vainlove! Then 'tis too late to dissemble. [Aside.] 'Tis plain, then, you have mistaken the person.

[Going.]

BELLMOUR

If we part so I'm mistaken. Hold, hold, madam! I confess I have run into an error. I beg your pardon a thousand times. What an eternal blockhead am I! Can you forgive me the disorder I have put you into? But it is a mistake which anybody might have made.

LÆTITIA

What can this mean? 'Tis impossible he should be mistaken after all this. A handsome fellow if he had not surprised me. Methinks, now I look on him again, I would not have him mistaken. [Aside.] We are all liable to mistakes, sir. If you own it to be so, there needs no farther apology.

BELLMOUR

Nay, faith, madam, 'tis a pleasant one, and worth your hearing. Expecting a friend last night, at his lodgings, till 'twas late, my intimacy with him gave me the freedom of his bed. He not coming home all night, a letter was delivered to me by a servant in the morning. Upon the perusal I found the contents so charming that I could think of nothing all day but putting 'em in practice, until just now, the first time I ever looked upon the superscription, I am the most surprised in the world to find it directed to Mr. Vainlove. Gad, madam, I ask you a million of pardons, and will make you any satisfaction.

LÆTITIA [Aside.]
I am discovered. And either Vainlove is not guilty, or he has handsomely excused him.

BELLMOUR
You appear concerned, madam.

LÆTITIA
I hope you are a gentleman;—and since you are privy to a weak woman's failing, won't turn it to the prejudice of her reputation. You look as if you had more honour—

BELLMOUR
And more love, or my face is a false witness and deserves to be pilloried. No, by heaven, I swear—

LÆTITIA
Nay, don't swear if you'd have me believe you; but promise—

BELLMOUR
Well, I promise. A promise is so cold: give me leave to swear, by those eyes, those killing eyes, by those healing lips. Oh! press the soft charm close to mine, and seal 'em up for ever.

LÆTITIA
Upon that condition.

[He kisses her.]

BELLMOUR
Eternity was in that moment. One more, upon any condition!

LÆTITIA
Nay, now—I never saw anything so agreeably impudent. [Aside.] Won't you censure me for this, now?—but 'tis to buy your silence.

[Kiss.]

Oh, but what am I doing!

BELLMOUR
Doing! No tongue can express it—not thy own, nor anything, but thy lips. I am faint with the excess of bliss. Oh, for love-sake, lead me any whither, where I may lie down—quickly, for I'm afraid I shall have a fit.

LÆTITIA
Bless me! What fit?

BELLMOUR
Oh, a convulsion—I feel the symptoms.

LÆTITIA

Does it hold you long? I'm afraid to carry you into my chamber.

BELLMOUR

Oh, no: let me lie down upon the bed; the fit will be soon over.

SCENE VIII. St. James's Park

ARAMINTA and **BELINDA** meeting.

BELINDA

Lard, my dear, I am glad I have met you; I have been at the Exchange since, and am so tired—

ARAMINTA

Why, what's the matter?

BELINDA

Oh the most inhuman, barbarous hackney-coach! I am jolted to a jelly. Am I not horribly touzed?

[Pulls out a pocket-glass.]

ARAMINTA

Your head's a little out of order.

BELINDA

A little! O frightful! What a furious phiz I have! O most rueful! Ha, ha, ha. O Gad, I hope nobody will come this way, till I have put myself a little in repair. Ah! my dear, I have seen such unhewn creatures since. Ha, ha, ha. I can't for my soul help thinking that I look just like one of 'em. Good dear, pin this, and I'll tell you—very well—so, thank you, my dear—but as I was telling you—pish, this is the untowardest lock—so, as I was telling you—how d'ye like me now? Hideous, ha? Frightful still? Or how?

ARAMINTA

No, no; you're very well as can be.

BELINDA

And so—but where did I leave off, my dear? I was telling you—

ARAMINTA

You were about to tell me something, child, but you left off before you began.

BELINDA

Oh; a most comical sight: a country squire, with the equipage of a wife and two daughters, came to Mrs. Snipwel's shop while I was there—but oh Gad! two such unlicked cubs!

ARAMINTA

I warrant, plump, cherry-cheeked country girls.

BELINDA

Ay, o' my conscience, fat as barn-door fowl: but so bedecked, you would have taken 'em for Friesland hens, with their feathers growing the wrong way. O such outlandish creatures! Such Tramontanæ, and foreigners to the fashion, or anything in practice! I had not patience to behold. I undertook the modelling of one of their fronts, the more modern structure—

ARAMINTA

Bless me, cousin; why would you affront anybody so? They might be gentlewomen of a very good family—

BELINDA

Of a very ancient one, I dare swear, by their dress. Affront! pshaw, how you're mistaken! The poor creature, I warrant, was as full of curtsies, as if I had been her godmother. The truth on't is, I did endeavour to make her look like a Christian—and she was sensible of it, for she thanked me, and gave me two apples, piping hot, out of her under-petticoat pocket. Ha, ha, ha: and t'other did so stare and gape, I fancied her like the front of her father's hall; her eyes were the two jut-windows, and her mouth the great door, most hospitably kept open for the entertainment of travelling flies.

ARAMINTA

So then, you have been diverted. What did they buy?

BELINDA

Why, the father bought a powder-horn, and an almanac, and a comb-case; the mother, a great fruz-towr, and a fat amber necklace; the daughters only tore two pairs of kid-leather gloves, with trying 'em on. O Gad, here comes the fool that dined at my Lady Freelove's t'other day.

SCENE IX

[To them **SIR JOSEPH WITTOLL** and **CAPTAIN BLUFFE**.

ARAMINTA

May be he may not know us again.

BELINDA

We'll put on our masks to secure his ignorance.

[They put on their masks.]

SIR JOSEPH WITTOLL

Nay, Gad, I'll pick up; I'm resolved to make a night on't. I'll go to Alderman Fondlewife by and by, and get fifty pieces more from him. Adslidikins, bully, we'll wallow in wine and women. Why, this same Madeira wine has made me as light as a grasshopper. Hist, hist, bully, dost thou see those tearers? [Sings.]
Look you what here is—look you what here is—toll—loll—dera—toll—loll—agad, t'other glass of Madeira, and I durst have attacked 'em in my own proper person, without your help.

CAPTAIN BLUFFE

Come on then, knight. But do you know what to say to them?

SIR JOSEPH WITTOLL

Say: pooh, pox, I've enough to say—never fear it—that is, if I can but think on't: truth is, I have but a treacherous memory.

BELINDA

O frightful! cousin, what shall we do? These things come towards us.

ARAMINTA

No matter. I see Vainlove coming this way—and, to confess my failing, I am willing to give him an opportunity of making his peace with me—and to rid me of these coxcombs, when I seem opprest with 'em, will be a fair one.

CAPTAIN BLUFFE

Ladies, by these hilts you are well met.

ARAMINTA

We are afraid not.

CAPTAIN BLUFFE

What says my pretty little knapsack carrier. [To **BELINDA**]

BELINDA

O monstrous filthy fellow! good slovenly Captain Huffe, Bluffe, what is your hideous name? be gone: you stink of brandy and tobacco, most soldier-like. Foh.

[Spits.]

SIR JOSEPH WITTOLL [Aside]

Now am I slap-dash down in the mouth, and have not one word to say!

ARAMINTA [Aside]

I hope my fool has not confidence enough to be troublesome.

SIR JOSEPH WITTOLL

Hem! Pray, madam, which way is the wind?

ARAMINTA

A pithy question. Have you sent your wits for a venture, sir, that you enquire?

SIR JOSEPH WITTOLL [Aside]

Nay, now I'm in, I can prattle like a magpie.

[To them **SHARPER** and **VAINLOVE** at some distance.

BELINDA
Dear Araminta, I'm tired.

ARAMINTA
'Tis but pulling off our masks, and obliging Vainlove to know us. I'll be rid of my fool by fair means.—
Well, Sir Joseph, you shall see my face; but, be gone immediately. I see one that will be jealous, to find
me in discourse with you. Be discreet. No reply; but away.

[Unmasks.]

SIR JOSEPH WITTOLL
The great fortune, that dined at my Lady Freelove's! Sir Joseph, thou art a made man. Agad, I'm in love
up to the ears. But I'll be discreet, and hushed. [Aside.]

CAPTAIN BLUFFE
Nay, by the world, I'll see your face.

BELINDA
You shall.

[Unmasks.]

SHARPER
Ladies, your humble servant. We were afraid you would not have given us leave to know you.

ARAMINTA
We thought to have been private. But we find fools have the same advantage over a face in a mask that
a coward has while the sword is in the scabbard, so were forced to draw in our own defence.

CAPTAIN BLUFFE
My blood rises at that fellow: I can't stay where he is; and I must not draw in the park. [To **SIR JOSEPH
WITTOLL**]

SIR JOSEPH WITTOLL
I wish I durst stay to let her know my lodging.

SCENE XI

ARAMINTA, BELINDA, VAINLOVE, SHARPER.

SHARPER

There is in true beauty, as in courage, somewhat which narrow souls cannot dare to admire. And see, the owls are fled, as at the break of day.

BELINDA
Very courtly. I believe Mr. Vainlove has not rubbed his eyes since break of day neither, he looks as if he durst not approach. Nay, come, cousin, be friends with him. I swear he looks so very simply—ha, ha, ha. Well, a lover in the state of separation from his mistress is like a body without a soul. Mr. Vainlove, shall I be bound for your good behaviour for the future?

VAINLOVE
Now must I pretend ignorance equal to hers, of what she knows as well as I. [Aside.] Men are apt to offend, 'tis true, where they find most goodness to forgive. But, madam, I hope I shall prove of a temper not to abuse mercy by committing new offences.

ARAMINTA [Aside.]
So cold!

BELINDA
I have broke the ice for you, Mr. Vainlove, and so I leave you. Come, Mr. Sharper, you and I will take a turn, and laugh at the vulgar—both the great vulgar and the small. O Gad! I have a great passion for Cowley. Don't you admire him?

SHARPER
Oh, madam! he was our English Horace.

BELINDA
Ah so fine! so extremely fine! So everything in the world that I like—O Lord, walk this way—I see a couple; I'll give you their history.

SCENE XII

ARAMINTA, VAINLOVE.

VAINLOVE
I find, madam, the formality of the law must be observed, though the penalty of it be dispensed with, and an offender must plead to his arraignment, though he has his pardon in his pocket.

ARAMINTA
I'm amazed! This insolence exceeds t'other; whoever has encouraged you to this assurance, presuming upon the easiness of my temper, has much deceived you, and so you shall find.

VAINLOVE [Aside.]
Hey day! Which way now? Here's fine doubling.

ARAMINTA
Base man! Was it not enough to affront me with your saucy passion?

VAINLOVE

You have given that passion a much kinder epithet than saucy, in another place.

ARAMINTA

Another place! Some villainous design to blast my honour. But though thou hadst all the treachery and malice of thy sex, thou canst not lay a blemish on my fame. No, I have not erred in one favourable thought of mankind. How time might have deceived me in you, I know not; my opinion was but young, and your early baseness has prevented its growing to a wrong belief. Unworthy and ungrateful! be gone, and never see me more.

VAINLOVE

Did I dream? or do I dream? Shall I believe my eyes, or ears? The vision is here still. Your passion, madam, will admit of no farther reasoning; but here's a silent witness of your acquaintance.

[Takes out the letter, and offers it: she snatches it, and throws it away.]

ARAMINTA

There's poison in everything you touch. Blisters will follow—

VAINLOVE

That tongue, which denies what the hands have done.

ARAMINTA

Still mystically senseless and impudent; I find I must leave the place.

VAINLOVE

No, madam, I'm gone. She knows her name's to it, which she will be unwilling to expose to the censure of the first finder.

ARAMINTA

Woman's obstinacy made me blind to what woman's curiosity now tempts me to see.

[Takes up the letter.]

SCENE XIII

BELINDA, SHARPER.

BELINDA

Nay, we have spared nobody, I swear. Mr. Sharper, you're a pure man; where did you get this excellent talent of railing?

SHARPER

Faith, madam, the talent was born with me:—I confess I have taken care to improve it, to qualify me for the society of ladies.

BELINDA
Nay, sure, railing is the best qualification in a woman's man.

SCENE XIV

[To them **FOOTMAN**.

SHARPER
The second best, indeed, I think.

BELINDA
How now, Pace? Where's my cousin?

FOOTMAN
She's not very well, madam, and has sent to know if your ladyship would have the coach come again for you?

BELINDA
O Lord, no, I'll go along with her. Come, Mr. Sharper.

SCENE XV. A Chamber in Fondlewife's House

LÆTITIA and BELLMOUR, his cloak, hat, etc., lying loose about the chamber.

BELLMOUR
Here's nobody, nor no noise—'twas nothing but your fears.

LÆTITIA
I durst have sworn I had heard my monster's voice. I swear I was heartily frightened; feel how my heart beats.

BELLMOUR
'Tis an alarm to love—come in again, and let us—

FONDLEWIFE [Without.]
Cocky, Cocky, where are you, Cocky? I'm come home.

LÆTITIA
Ah! There he is. Make haste, gather up your things.

FONDLEWIFE
Cocky, Cocky, open the door.

BELLMOUR

Pox choke him, would his horns were in his throat. My patch, my patch.

[Looking about, and gathering up his things.]

LÆTITIA

My jewel, art thou there?—No matter for your patch.—You s'an't tum in, Nykin—run into my chamber, quickly, quickly—You s'an't tum in.

FONDLEWIFE

Nay, prithee, dear, i'feck I'm in haste.

LÆTITIA

Then I'll let you in.

[Opens the door.]

SCENE XVI

LÆTITIA, FONDLEWIFE, SIR JOSEPH.

FONDLEWIFE

Kiss, dear—I met the master of the ship by the way, and I must have my papers of accounts out of your cabinet.

LÆTITIA [Aside.]
Oh, I'm undone!

SIR JOSEPH WITTOLL

Pray, first let me have fifty pound, good Alderman, for I'm in haste.

FONDLEWIFE

A hundred has already been paid by your order. Fifty? I have the sum ready in gold in my closet.

SCENE XVII

LÆTITIA, SIR JOSEPH WITTOLL.

SIR JOSEPH WITTOLL

Agad, it's a curious, fine, pretty rogue; I'll speak to her.—Pray, Madam, what news d'ye hear?

LÆTITIA

Sir, I seldom stir abroad.

[Walks about in disorder.]

SIR JOSEPH WITTOLL
I wonder at that, Madam, for 'tis most curious fine weather.

LÆTITIA
Methinks 't has been very ill weather.

SIR JOSEPH WITTOLL
As you say, madam, 'tis pretty bad weather, and has been so a great while.

SCENE XVIII

[To them **FONDLEWIFE**.

FONDLEWIFE
Here are fifty pieces in this purse, Sir Joseph; if you will tarry a moment, till I fetch my papers, I'll wait upon you down-stairs.

LÆTITIA
Ruined, past redemption! what shall I do—ha! this fool may be of use. (Aside.)

[As **FONDLEWIFE** is going into the chamber, she runs to **SIR JOSEPH WITTOLL,** almost pushes him down, and cries out.]

Stand off, rude ruffian. Help me, my dear. O bless me! Why will you leave me alone with such a Satyr?

FONDLEWIFE
Bless us! What's the matter? What's the matter?

LÆTITIA
Your back was no sooner turned, but like a lion he came open mouthed upon me, and would have ravished a kiss from me by main force.

SIR JOSEPH WITTOLL
O Lord! Oh, terrible! Ha, ha, ha. Is your wife mad, Alderman?

LÆTITIA
Oh! I'm sick with the fright; won't you take him out of my sight?

FONDLEWIFE
O traitor! I'm astonished. O bloody-minded traitor!

SIR JOSEPH WITTOLL
Hey-day! Traitor yourself. By the Lord Harry, I was in most danger of being ravished, if you go to that.

FONDLEWIFE

Oh, how the blasphemous wretch swears! Out of my house, thou son of the whore of Babylon; offspring of Bel and the Dragon.—Bless us! ravish my wife! my Dinah! Oh, Shechemite! Begone, I say.

SIR JOSEPH WITTOLL

Why, the devil's in the people, I think.

SCENE XIX

LÆTITIA, FONDLEWIFE.

LÆTITIA

Oh! won't you follow, and see him out of doors, my dear?

FONDLEWIFE

I'll shut this door to secure him from coming back—Give me the key of your cabinet, Cocky. Ravish my wife before my face? I warrant he's a Papist in his heart at least, if not a Frenchman.

LÆTITIA

What can I do now! (Aside.) Oh! my dear, I have been in such a fright, that I forgot to tell you, poor Mr. Spintext has a sad fit of the colic, and is forced to lie down upon our bed—you'll disturb him; I can tread softlier.

FONDLEWIFE

Alack, poor man—no, no—you don't know the papers—I won't disturb him; give me the key.

[She gives him the key, goes to the chamber door and speaks aloud.]

LÆTITIA

'Tis nobody but Mr. Fondlewife, Mr. Spintext, lie still on your stomach; lying on your stomach will ease you of the colic.

FONDLEWIFE

Ay, ay, lie still, lie still; don't let me disturb you.

SCENE XX

LÆTITIA alone.

LÆTITIA

Sure, when he does not see his face, he won't discover him. Dear fortune, help me but this once, and I'll never run in thy debt again. But this opportunity is the Devil.

FONDLEWIFE returns with Papers.

FONDLEWIFE

Good lack! good lack! I profess the poor man is in great torment; he lies as flat—Dear, you should heat a trencher, or a napkin.—Where's Deborah? Let her clap some warm thing to his stomach, or chafe it with a warm hand rather than fail. What book's this?

[Sees the book that **BELLMOUR** forgot.]

LÆTITIA

Mr. Spintext's prayer-book, dear. Pray Heaven it be a prayer-book. [Aside.]

FONDLEWIFE

Good man! I warrant he dropped it on purpose that you might take it up and read some of the pious ejaculations.

[Taking up the book.]

O bless me! O monstrous! A prayer-book? Ay, this is the devil's paternoster. Hold, let me see: The Innocent Adultery.

LÆTITIA [Aside.]
Misfortune! now all's ruined again.

BELLMOUR [Peeping].
Damned chance! If I had gone a-whoring with the Practice of Piety in my pocket I had never been discovered.

FONDLEWIFE

Adultery, and innocent! O Lord! Here's doctrine! Ay, here's discipline!

LÆTITIA

Dear husband, I'm amazed. Sure it is a good book, and only tends to the speculation of sin.

FONDLEWIFE

Speculation! No no; something went farther than speculation when I was not to be let in.—Where is this apocryphal elder? I'll ferret him.

LÆTITIA [Aside.]
I'm so distracted, I can't think of a lie.

LÆTITIA and **FONDLEWIFE** haling out **BELLMOUR**.

FONDLEWIFE
Come out here, thou Ananias incarnate. Who, how now! Who have we here?

LÆTITIA [Shrieks as surprised.]
Ha!

FONDLEWIFE
Oh thou salacious woman! Am I then brutified? Ay, I feel it here; I sprout, I bud, I blossom, I am ripe-horn-mad. But who in the devil's name are you? Mercy on me for swearing. But—

LÆTITIA
Oh! goodness keep us! Who are you? What are you?

BELLMOUR
Soh!

LÆTITIA
In the name of the—O! Good, my dear, don't come near it; I'm afraid 'tis the devil; indeed, it has hoofs, dear.

FONDLEWIFE
Indeed, and I have horns, dear. The devil, no, I am afraid 'tis the flesh, thou harlot. Dear, with the pox. Come Syren, speak, confess, who is this reverend, brawny pastor.

LÆTITIA
Indeed, and indeed now, my dear Nykin, I never saw this wicked man before.

FONDLEWIFE
Oh, it is a man then, it seems.

LÆTITIA
Rather, sure it is a wolf in the clothing of a sheep.

FONDLEWIFE
Thou art a devil in his proper clothing—woman's flesh. What, you know nothing of him, but his fleece here! You don't love mutton? you Magdalen unconverted.

BELLMOUR
Well, now, I know my cue.—That is, very honourably to excuse her, and very impudently accuse myself. [Aside.]

LÆTITIA
Why then, I wish I may never enter into the heaven of your embraces again, my dear, if ever I saw his face before.

FONDLEWIFE

O Lord! O strange! I am in admiration of your impudence. Look at him a little better; he is more modest, I warrant you, than to deny it. Come, were you two never face to face before? Speak.

BELLMOUR
Since all artifice is **VAINLOVE**
And I think myself obliged to speak the truth in justice to your wife.—No.

FONDLEWIFE
Humph.

LÆTITIA
No, indeed, dear.

FONDLEWIFE
Nay, I find you are both in a story; that I must confess. But, what—not to be cured of the colic? Don't you know your patient, Mrs. Quack? Oh, 'lie upon your stomach; lying upon your stomach will cure you of the colic.' Ah! answer me, Jezebel?

LÆTITIA
Let the wicked man answer for himself: does he think I have nothing to do but excuse him? 'tis enough if I can clear my own innocence to my own dear.

BELLMOUR
By my troth, and so 'tis. I have been a little too backward; that's the truth on't.

FONDLEWIFE
Come, sir, who are you, in the first place? And what are you?

BELLMOUR
A whore-master.

FONDLEWIFE
Very concise.

LÆTITIA
O beastly, impudent creature.

FONDLEWIFE
Well, sir, and what came you hither for?

BELLMOUR
To lie with your wife.

FONDLEWIFE
Good again. A very civil person this, and I believe speaks truth.

LÆTITIA
Oh, insupportable impudence.

FONDLEWIFE

Well, sir; pray be covered—and you have—Heh! You have finished the matter, heh? And I am, as I should be, a sort of civil perquisite to a whore-master, called a cuckold, heh? Is it not so? Come, I'm inclining to believe every word you say.

BELLMOUR

Why, faith, I must confess, so I designed you; but you were a little unlucky in coming so soon, and hindered the making of your own fortune.

FONDLEWIFE

Humph. Nay, if you mince the matter once and go back of your word you are not the person I took you for. Come, come, go on boldly.—What, don't be ashamed of your profession.—Confess, confess; I shall love thee the better for't. I shall, i'feck. What, dost think I don't know how to behave myself in the employment of a cuckold, and have been three years apprentice to matrimony? Come, come; plain dealing is a jewel.

BELLMOUR

Well, since I see thou art a good, honest fellow, I'll confess the whole matter to thee.

FONDLEWIFE

Oh, I am a very honest fellow. You never lay with an honester man's wife in your life.

LÆTITIA

How my heart aches! All my comfort lies in his impudence, and heaven be praised, he has a considerable portion. [Aside.]

BELLMOUR

In short, then, I was informed of the opportunity of your absence by my spy, for faith, honest Isaac, I have a long time designed thee this favour. I knew Spintext was to come by your direction. But I laid a trap for him, and procured his habit, in which I passed upon your servants, and was conducted hither. I pretended a fit of the colic, to excuse my lying down upon your bed; hoping that when she heard of it, her good nature would bring her to administer remedies for my distemper. You know what might have followed. But, like an uncivil person, you knocked at the door before your wife was come to me.

FONDLEWIFE

Ha! This is apocryphal; I may choose whether I will believe it or no.

BELLMOUR

That you may, faith, and I hope you won't believe a word on't—but I can't help telling the truth, for my life.

FONDLEWIFE

How! would not you have me believe you, say you?

BELLMOUR

No; for then you must of consequence part with your wife, and there will be some hopes of having her upon the public; then the encouragement of a separate maintenance—

FONDLEWIFE
No, no; for that matter, when she and I part, she'll carry her separate maintenance about her.

LÆTITIA
Ah, cruel dear, how can you be so barbarous? You'll break my heart, if you talk of parting.

[Cries.]

FONDLEWIFE
Ah, dissembling vermin!

BELLMOUR
How can'st thou be so cruel, Isaac? Thou hast the heart of a mountain-tiger. By the faith of a sincere sinner, she's innocent for me. Go to him, madam, fling your snowy arms about his stubborn neck; bathe his relentless face in your salt trickling tears.

[She goes and hangs upon his neck, and kisses him. **BELLMOUR** kisses her hand behind **FONDLEWIFE'S** back.]

So, a few soft words, and a kiss, and the good man melts. See how kind nature works, and boils over in him.

LÆTITIA
Indeed, my dear, I was but just come down stairs, when you knocked at the door; and the maid told me Mr. Spintext was ill of the colic upon our bed. And won't you speak to me, cruel Nykin? Indeed, I'll die, if you don't.

FONDLEWIFE
Ah! No, no, I cannot speak, my heart's so full—I have been a tender husband, a tender yoke-fellow; you know I have.—But thou hast been a faithless Delilah, and the Philistines—Heh! Art thou not vile and unclean, heh? Speak.

[Weeping.]

LÆTITIA [Sighing.]
No-h.

FONDLEWIFE
Oh that I could believe thee!

LÆTITIA
Oh, my heart will break.

[Seeming to faint.]

FONDLEWIFE
Heh, how! No, stay, stay, I will believe thee, I will. Pray bend her forward, sir.

LÆTITIA

Oh! oh! Where is my dear?

FONDLEWIFE

Here, here; I do believe thee. I won't believe my own eyes.

BELLMOUR

For my part, I am so charmed with the love of your turtle to you, that I'll go and solicit matrimony with all my might and main.

FONDLEWIFE

Well, well, sir; as long as I believe it, 'tis well enough. No thanks to you, sir, for her virtue.—But, I'll show you the way out of my house, if you please. Come, my dear. Nay, I will believe thee, I do, i'feck.

BELLMOUR

See the great blessing of an easy faith; opinion cannot err.

No husband, by his wife, can be deceived; She still is virtuous, if she's so believed.

ACT V

SCENE I. The Street

BELLMOUR in fanatic habit, **SETTER, HEARTWELL, LUCY**.

BELLMOUR

Setter! Well encountered.

SETTER

Joy of your return, sir. Have you made a good voyage? or have you brought your own lading back?

BELLMOUR

No, I have brought nothing but ballast back—made a delicious voyage, Setter; and might have rode at anchor in the port till this time, but the enemy surprised us—I would unrig.

SETTER

I attend you, sir.

BELLMOUR

Ha! Is it not that Heartwell at Sylvia's door? Be gone quickly, I'll follow you—I would not be known. Pox take 'em, they stand just in my way.

SCENE II

BELLMOUR, HEARTWELL, LUCY.

HEARTWELL
I'm impatient till it be done.

LUCY
That may be, without troubling yourself to go again for your brother's chaplain. Don't you see that stalking form of godliness?

HEARTWELL
O ay; he's a fanatic.

LUCY
An executioner qualified to do your business. He has been lawfully ordained.

HEARTWELL
I'll pay him well, if you'll break the matter to him.

LUCY
I warrant you.—Do you go and prepare your bride.

SCENE III

BELLMOUR, LUCY.

BELLMOUR
Humph, sits the wind there? What a lucky rogue am I! Oh, what sport will be here, if I can persuade this wench to secrecy!

LUCY
Sir: reverend sir.

BELLMOUR
Madam.

[Discovers himself.]

LUCY
Now, goodness have mercy upon me! Mr. Bellmour! is it you?

BELLMOUR
Even I. What dost think?

LUCY
Think! That I should not believe my eyes, and that you are not what you seem to be.

BELLMOUR

True. But to convince thee who I am, thou knowest my old token.

[Kisses her.]

LUCY

Nay, Mr. Bellmour: O Lard! I believe you are a parson in good earnest, you kiss so devoutly.

BELLMOUR

Well, your business with me, Lucy?

LUCY

I had none, but through mistake.

BELLMOUR

Which mistake you must go through with, Lucy. Come, I know the intrigue between Heartwell and your mistress; and you mistook me for Tribulation Spintext, to marry 'em—Ha? are not matters in this posture? Confess: come, I'll be faithful; I will, i'faith. What! diffide in me, Lucy?

LUCY

Alas-a-day! You and Mr. Vainlove, between you, have ruined my poor mistress: you have made a gap in her reputation; and can you blame her if she make it up with a husband?

BELLMOUR

Well, is it as I say?

LUCY

Well, it is then: but you'll be secret?

BELLMOUR

Phuh, secret, ay. And to be out of thy debt, I'll trust thee with another secret. Your mistress must not marry Heartwell, Lucy.

LUCY

How! O Lord!

BELLMOUR

Nay, don't be in passion, Lucy:—I'll provide a fitter husband for her. Come, here's earnest of my good intentions for thee too; let this mollify.

[Gives her money.]

Look you, Heartwell is my friend; and though he be blind, I must not see him fall into the snare, and unwittingly marry a whore.

LUCY

Whore! I'd have you to know my mistress scorns—

BELLMOUR

Nay, nay: look you, Lucy; there are whores of as good quality. But to the purpose, if you will give me leave to acquaint you with it. Do you carry on the mistake of me: I'll marry 'em. Nay, don't pause; if you do, I'll spoil all. I have some private reasons for what I do, which I'll tell you within. In the meantime, I promise—and rely upon me—to help your mistress to a husband: nay, and thee too, Lucy. Here's my hand, I will; with a fresh assurance.

[Gives her more money.]

LUCY

Ah, the devil is not so cunning. You know my easy nature. Well, for once I'll venture to serve you; but if you do deceive me, the curse of all kind, tender-hearted women light upon you!

BELLMOUR

That's as much as to say, the pox take me. Well, lead on.

SCENE IV

VAINLOVE, SHARPER, and SETTER.

SHARPER

Just now, say you; gone in with Lucy?

SETTER

I saw him, sir, and stood at the corner where you found me, and overheard all they said: Mr. Bellmour is to marry 'em.

SHARPER

Ha, ha; it will be a pleasant cheat. I'll plague Heartwell when I see him. Prithee, Frank, let's tease him; make him fret till he foam at the mouth, and disgorge his matrimonial oath with interest. Come, thou'rt musty—

SETTER [To **SHARPER**]

Sir, a word with you. [Whispers him.]

VAINLOVE

Sharper swears she has forsworn the letter—I'm sure he tells me truth;—but I'm not sure she told him truth: yet she was unaffectedly concerned, he says, and often blushed with anger and surprise: and so I remember in the park. She had reason, if I wrong her. I begin to doubt.

SHARPER

Say'st thou so?

SETTER

This afternoon, sir, about an hour before my master received the letter.

SHARPER

In my conscience, like enough.

SETTER

Ay, I know her, sir; at least, I'm sure I can fish it out of her: she's the very sluice to her lady's secrets: 'tis but setting her mill agoing, and I can drain her of 'em all.

SHARPER

Here, Frank, your bloodhound has made out the fault: this letter, that so sticks in thy maw, is counterfeit; only a trick of Sylvia in revenge, contrived by Lucy.

VAINLOVE

Ha! It has a colour; but how do you know it, sirrah?

SETTER

I do suspect as much; because why, sir, she was pumping me about how your worship's affairs stood towards Madam Araminta; as, when you had seen her last? when you were to see her next? and, where you were to be found at that time? and such like.

VAINLOVE

And where did you tell her?

SETTER

In the Piazza.

VAINLOVE

There I received the letter—it must be so—and why did you not find me out, to tell me this before, sot?

SETTER

Sir, I was pimping for Mr. Bellmour.

SHARPER

You were well employed: I think there is no objection to the excuse.

VAINLOVE

Pox of my saucy credulity—if I have lost her, I deserve it. But if confession and repentance be of force, I'll win her, or weary her into a forgiveness.

SHARPER

Methinks I long to see Bellmour come forth.

SCENE V

SHARPER, BELLMOUR, SETTER.

SETTER

Talk of the devil: see where he comes.

SHARPER

Hugging himself in his prosperous mischief—no real fanatic can look better pleased after a successful sermon of sedition.

BELLMOUR

Sharper! Fortify thy spleen: such a jest! Speak when thou art ready.

SHARPER

Now, were I ill-natured would I utterly disappoint thy mirth: hear thee tell thy mighty jest with as much gravity as a bishop hears venereal causes in the spiritual court. Not so much as wrinkle my face with one smile; but let thee look simply, and laugh by thyself.

BELLMOUR

Pshaw, no; I have a better opinion of thy wit. Gad, I defy thee.

SHARPER

Were it not loss of time you should make the experiment. But honest Setter, here, overheard you with Lucy, and has told me all.

BELLMOUR

Nay, then, I thank thee for not putting me out of countenance. But, to tell you something you don't know. I got an opportunity after I had married 'em, of discovering the cheat to Sylvia. She took it at first, as another woman would the like disappointment; but my promise to make her amends quickly with another husband somewhat pacified her.

SHARPER

But how the devil do you think to acquit yourself of your promise? Will you marry her yourself?

BELLMOUR

I have no such intentions at present. Prithee, wilt thou think a little for me? I am sure the ingenious Mr. Setter will assist.

SETTER

O Lord, sir!

BELLMOUR

I'll leave him with you, and go shift my habit.

SCENE VI

SHARPER, SETTER, SIR JOSEPH WITTOLL, and **CAPTAIN BLUFFE.**

SHARPER

Heh! Sure fortune has sent this fool hither on purpose. Setter, stand close; seem not to observe 'em; and, hark ye. [Whispers.]

CAPTAIN BLUFFE
Fear him not. I am prepared for him now, and he shall find he might have safer roused a sleeping lion.

SIR JOSEPH WITTOLL
Hush, hush! don't you see him?

CAPTAIN BLUFFE
Show him to me. Where is he?

SIR JOSEPH WITTOLL
Nay, don't speak so loud. I don't jest as I did a little while ago. Look yonder! Agad, if he should hear the lion roar, he'd cudgel him into an ass, and his primitive braying. Don't you remember the story in Æsop's Fables, bully? Agad, there are good morals to be picked out of Æsop's Fables, let me tell you that, and Reynard the Fox too.

CAPTAIN BLUFFE
Damn your morals.

SIR JOSEPH WITTOLL
Prithee, don't speak so loud.

CAPTAIN BLUFFE [In a low voice.]
Damn your morals; I must revenge the affront done to my honour.

SIR JOSEPH WITTOLL
Ay; do, do, captain, if you think fitting. You may dispose of your own flesh as you think fitting, d'ye see, but, by the Lord Harry, I'll leave you.

[Stealing away upon his tip-toes.]

CAPTAIN BLUFFE
Prodigious! What, will you forsake your friend in extremity? You can't in honour refuse to carry him a challenge.

[Almost whispering, and treading softly after him.]

SIR JOSEPH WITTOLL
Prithee, what do you see in my face that looks as if I would carry a challenge? Honour is your province, captain; take it. All the world know me to be a knight, and a man of worship.

SETTER
I warrant you, sir, I'm instructed.

SHARPER [Aloud.]
Impossible! Araminta take a liking to a fool?

SETTER

Her head runs on nothing else, nor she can talk of nothing else.

SHARPER

I know she commanded him all the while we were in the Park; but I thought it had been only to make Vainlove jealous.

SIR JOSEPH WITTOLL

How's this! Good bully, hold your breath and let's hearken. Agad, this must be I.

SHARPER

Death, it can't be. An oaf, an idiot, a wittal.

SIR JOSEPH WITTOLL

Ay, now it's out; 'tis I, my own individual person.

SHARPER

A wretch that has flown for shelter to the lowest shrub of mankind, and seeks protection from a blasted coward.

SIR JOSEPH WITTOLL

That's you, bully back.

[**CAPTAIN BLUFFE** frowns upon **SIR JOSEPH WITTOLL.**]

SHARPER

She has given Vainlove her promise to marry him before to-morrow morning. Has she not? [To **SETTER.**]

SETTER

She has, sir; and I have it in charge to attend her all this evening, in order to conduct her to the place appointed.

SHARPER

Well, I'll go and inform your master; and do you press her to make all the haste imaginable.

SCENE VII

SETTER, SIR JOSEPH WITTOLL, CAPTAIN BLUFFE.

SETTER

Were I a rogue now, what a noble prize could I dispose of! A goodly pinnace, richly laden, and to launch forth under my auspicious convoy. Twelve thousand pounds and all her rigging, besides what lies concealed under hatches. Ha! all this committed to my care! Avaunt, temptation! Setter, show thyself a person of worth; be true to thy trust, and be reputed honest. Reputed honest! Hum: is that all? Ay; for to be honest is nothing; the reputation of it is all. Reputation! what have such poor rogues as I to do with reputation? 'tis above us; and for men of quality, they are above it; so that reputation is even as foolish a thing as honesty. And, for my part, if I meet Sir Joseph with a purse of gold in his hand, I'll dispose of mine to the best advantage.

SIR JOSEPH WITTOLL
Heh, heh, heh: Here 'tis for you, i'faith, Mr. Setter. Nay, I'll take you at your word.

[Chinking a purse.]

SETTER
Sir Joseph and the captain, too! undone! undone! I'm undone, my master's undone, my lady's undone, and all the business is undone.

SIR JOSEPH WITTOLL
No, no; never fear, man; the lady's business shall be done. What, come, Mr. Setter, I have overheard all, and to speak is but loss of time; but if there be occasion, let these worthy gentlemen intercede for me.

[Gives him gold.]

SETTER
O lord, sir, what d'ye mean? Corrupt my honesty? They have indeed very persuading faces. But—

SIR JOSEPH WITTOLL
'Tis too little, there's more, man. There, take all. Now—

SETTER
Well, Sir Joseph, you have such a winning way with you—

SIR JOSEPH WITTOLL
And how, and how, good Setter, did the little rogue look when she talked of Sir Joseph? Did not her eyes twinkle and her mouth water? Did not she pull up her little bubbies? And—agad, I'm so overjoyed—And stroke down her belly? and then step aside to tie her garter when she was thinking of her love? Heh, Setter!

SETTER
Oh, yes, sir.

SIR JOSEPH WITTOLL
How now, bully? What, melancholy because I'm in the lady's favour? No matter, I'll make your peace: I know they were a little smart upon you. But I warrant I'll bring you into the lady's good graces.

CAPTAIN BLUFFE
Pshaw, I have petitions to show from other-guess toys than she. Look here; these were sent me this morning. There, read.

[Shows letters].

That—that's a scrawl of quality. Here, here's from a countess too. Hum—No, hold—that's from a knight's wife—she sent it me by her husband. But here, both these are from persons of great quality.

SIR JOSEPH WITTOLL
They are either from persons of great quality, or no quality at all, 'tis such a damned ugly hand.

[While **SIR JOSEPH WITTOLL** reads, **CAPTAIN BLUFFE** whispers **SETTER**.]

SETTER
Captain, I would do anything to serve you; but this is so difficult.

CAPTAIN BLUFFE
Not at all. Don't I know him?

SETTER
You'll remember the conditions?

CAPTAIN BLUFFE
I'll give it you under my hand. In the meantime, here's earnest.

[Gives him money.]

Come, knight, I'm capitulating with Mr. Setter for you.

SIR JOSEPH WITTOLL
Ah, honest Setter; sirrah, I'll give thee anything but a night's lodging.

SCENE VIII

SHARPER tugging in **HEARTWELL**.

SHARPER
Nay, prithee leave railing, and come along with me. May be she mayn't be within. 'Tis but to yond corner-house.

HEARTWELL
Whither? Whither? Which corner-house.

SHARPER
Why, there: the two white posts.

HEARTWELL
And who would you visit there, say you? O'ons, how my heart aches.

SHARPER

Pshaw, thou'rt so troublesome and inquisitive. My, I'll tell you; 'tis a young creature that Vainlove debauched and has forsaken. Did you never hear Bellmour chide him about Sylvia?

HEARTWELL
Death, and hell, and marriage! My wife! [Aside.]

SHARPER
Why, thou art as musty as a new-married man that had found his wife knowing the first night.

HEARTWELL
Hell, and the Devil! Does he know it? But, hold; if he should not, I were a fool to discover it. I'll dissemble, and try him. [Aside.] Ha, ha, ha. Why, Tom, is that such an occasion of melancholy? Is it such an uncommon mischief?

SHARPER
No, faith; I believe not. Few women but have their year of probation before they are cloistered in the narrow joys of wedlock. But, prithee, come along with me or I'll go and have the lady to myself. B'w'y George.

[Going.]

HEARTWELL
O torture! How he racks and tears me! Death! Shall I own my shame or wittingly let him go and whore my wife? No, that's insupportable. O Sharper!

SHARPER
How now?

HEARTWELL
Oh, I am married.

SHARPER
Now hold, spleen. Married!

HEARTWELL
Certainly, irrecoverably married.

SHARPER
Heaven forbid, man! How long?

HEARTWELL
Oh, an age, an age! I have been married these two hours.

SHARPER
My old bachelor married! That were a jest. Ha, ha, ha.

HEARTWELL

Death! D'ye mock me? Hark ye, if either you esteem my friendship, or your own safety—come not near that house—that corner-house—that hot brothel. Ask no questions.

SHARPER
Mad, by this light.
Thus grief still treads upon the heels of pleasure:
Married in haste, we may repent at leisure.

SCENE IX

SHARPER, SETTER.

SETTER
Some by experience find these words misplaced: At leisure married, they repent in haste.

As I suppose my master Heartwell.

SHARPER
Here again, my Mercury!

SETTER
Sublimate, if you please, sir: I think my achievements do deserve the epithet—Mercury was a pimp too, but, though I blush to own it, at this time, I must confess I am somewhat fallen from the dignity of my function, and do condescend to be scandalously employed in the promotion of vulgar matrimony.

SHARPER
As how, dear, dexterous pimp?

SETTER
Why, to be brief, for I have weighty affairs depending—our stratagem succeeded as you intended—Bluffe turns errant traitor; bribes me to make a private conveyance of the lady to him, and put a shame-settlement upon Sir Joseph.

SHARPER
O rogue! Well, but I hope—

SETTER
No, no; never fear me, sir. I privately informed the knight of the treachery, who has agreed seemingly to be cheated, that the captain may be so in reality.

SHARPER
Where's the bride?

SETTER
Shifting clothes for the purpose, at a friend's house of mine. Here's company coming; if you'll walk this way, sir, I'll tell you.

BELLMOUR, BELINDA, ARAMINTA, and **VAINLOVE.**

VAINLOVE
Oh, 'twas frenzy all: cannot you forgive it? Men in madness have a title to your pity. [To **ARAMINTA.**]

ARAMINTA
Which they forfeit, when they are restored to their senses.

VAINLOVE
I am not presuming beyond a pardon.

ARAMINTA
You who could reproach me with one counterfeit, how insolent would a real pardon make you! But there's no need to forgive what is not worth my anger.

BELINDA
O' my conscience, I could find in my heart to marry thee, purely to be rid of thee—at least thou art so troublesome a lover, there's hopes thou'lt make a more than ordinary quiet husband. [To **BELLMOUR**]

BELLMOUR
Say you so? Is that a maxim among ye?

BELINDA
Yes: you fluttering men of the mode have made marriage a mere French dish.

BELLMOUR [Aside.]
I hope there's no French sauce.

BELINDA
You are so curious in the preparation, that is, your courtship, one would think you meant a noble entertainment—but when we come to feed, 'tis all froth, and poor, but in show. Nay, often, only remains, which have been I know not how many times warmed for other company, and at last served up cold to the wife.

BELLMOUR
That were a miserable wretch indeed, who could not afford one warm dish for the wife of his bosom. But you timorous virgins form a dreadful chimæra of a husband, as of a creature contrary to that soft, humble, pliant, easy thing, a lover; so guess at plagues in matrimony, in opposition to the pleasures of courtship. Alas! courtship to marriage, is but as the music in the play-house, until the curtain's drawn; but that once up, then opens the scene of pleasure.

BELINDA
Oh, foh,—no: rather courtship to marriage, as a very witty prologue to a very dull play.

[To them **SHARPER**.

SHARPER
Hist! Bellmour. If you'll bring the ladies, make haste to Sylvia's lodgings, before Heartwell has fretted himself out of breath.

BELLMOUR
You have an opportunity now, madam, to revenge yourself upon Heartwell, for affronting your squirrel.
[To **BELINDA**]

BELINDA
Oh, the filthy rude beast.

ARAMINTA
'Tis a lasting quarrel; I think he has never been at our house since.

BELLMOUR
But give yourselves the trouble to walk to that corner-house, and I'll tell you by the way what may divert and surprise you.

SCENE XII. Sylvia's Lodgings

HEARTWELL and **BOY**.

HEARTWELL
Gone forth, say you, with her maid?

BOY
There was a man too, that fetched them out—Setter, I think they called him.

HEARTWELL
So-h—that precious pimp too—damned, damned strumpet! could she not contain herself on her wedding-day? not hold out till night? Oh, cursed state! how wide we err, when apprehensive of the load of life.

We hope to find That help which Nature meant in womankind, To man that supplemental self-designed; But proves a burning caustic when applied, And Adam, sure, could with more ease abide The bone when broken, than when made a bride.

[To him **BELLMOUR, BELINDA, VAINLOVE, ARAMINTA**.

BELLMOUR
Now George, what, rhyming! I thought the chimes of verse were past, when once the doleful marriage-knell was rung.

HEARTWELL
Shame and confusion, I am exposed.

[**VAINLOVE** and **ARAMINTA** talk apart.]

BELINDA
Joy, joy, Mr. Bridegroom; I give you joy, sir.

HEARTWELL
'Tis not in thy nature to give me joy. A woman can as soon give immortality.

BELINDA
Ha, ha, ha! oh Gad, men grow such clowns when they are married.

BELLMOUR
That they are fit for no company but their wives.

BELINDA
Nor for them neither, in a little time. I swear, at the month's end, you shall hardly find a married man that will do a civil thing to his wife, or say a civil thing to anybody else. How he looks already, ha, ha, ha.

BELLMOUR
Ha, ha, ha!

HEARTWELL
Death, am I made your laughing-stock? For you, sir, I shall find a time; but take off your wasp here, or the clown may grow boisterous; I have a fly-flap.

BELINDA
You have occasion for't, your wife has been blown upon.

BELLMOUR
That's home.

HEARTWELL
Not fiends or furies could have added to my vexation, or anything, but another woman. You've racked my patience; begone, or by—

BELLMOUR
Hold, hold. What the devil—thou wilt not draw upon a woman?

VAINLOVE
What's the matter?

ARAMINTA
Bless me! what have you done to him?

BELINDA
Only touched a galled beast until he winced.

VAINLOVE
Bellmour, give it over; you vex him too much. 'Tis all serious to him.

BELINDA
Nay, I swear, I begin to pity him myself.

HEARTWELL
Damn your pity!—but let me be calm a little. How have I deserved this of you? any of ye? Sir, have I impaired the honour of your house, promised your sister marriage, and whored her? Wherein have I injured you? Did I bring a physician to your father when he lay expiring, and endeavour to prolong his life, and you one and twenty? Madam, have I had an opportunity with you and baulked it? Did you ever offer me the favour that I refused it? Or—

BELINDA
Oh foh! what does the filthy fellow mean? Lord, let me be gone.

ARAMINTA
Hang me, if I pity you; you are right enough served.

BELLMOUR
This is a little scurrilous though.

VAINLOVE
Nay, 'tis a sore of your own scratching—well, George?

HEARTWELL
You are the principal cause of all my present ills. If Sylvia had not been your mistress, my wife might have been honest.

VAINLOVE
And if Sylvia had not been your wife, my mistress might have been just. There, we are even. But have a good heart, I heard of your misfortune, and come to your relief.

HEARTWELL
When execution's over, you offer a reprieve.

VAINLOVE
What would you give?

HEARTWELL

Oh! Anything, everything, a leg or two, or an arm; nay, I would be divorced from my virility to be divorced from my wife.

SCENE XIV

[To them **SHARPER**.

VAINLOVE

Faith, that's a sure way: but here's one can sell you freedom better cheap.

SHARPER

Vainlove, I have been a kind of a godfather to you yonder. I have promised and vowed some things in your name which I think you are bound to perform.

VAINLOVE

No signing to a blank, friend.

SHARPER

No, I'll deal fairly with you. 'Tis a full and free discharge to Sir Joseph Wittal and Captain Bluffe; for all injuries whatsoever, done unto you by them, until the present date hereof. How say you?

VAINLOVE

Agreed.

SHARPER

Then, let me beg these ladies to wear their masks, a moment. Come in, gentlemen and ladies.

HEARTWELL

What the devil's all this to me?

VAINLOVE

Patience.

SCENE the Last

[To them **SIR JOSEPH WITTOLL, BLUFFE, SYLVIA, LUCY, SETTER**.

CAPTAIN BLUFFE

All injuries whatsoever, Mr. Sharper.

SIR JOSEPH WITTOLL

Ay, ay, whatsoever, Captain, stick to that; whatsoever.

SHARPER

'Tis done, these gentlemen are witnesses to the general release.

VAINLOVE

Ay, ay, to this instant moment. I have passed an act of oblivion.

CAPTAIN BLUFFE

'Tis very generous, sir, since I needs must own—

SIR JOSEPH WITTOLL

No, no, Captain, you need not own, heh, heh, heh. 'Tis I must own—

CAPTIN BLUFFE

That you are over-reached too, ha, ha, ha, only a little art military used—only undermined, or so, as shall appear by the fair Araminta, my wife's permission. Oh, the devil, cheated at last!

[**LUCY** unmasks.]

SIR JOSEPH WITTOLL

Only a little art-military trick, captain, only countermined, or so. Mr. Vainlove, I suppose you know whom I have got—now, but all's forgiven.

VAINLOVE

I know whom you have not got; pray ladies convince him.

[**ARAMINTA** and **BELINDA** unmask.]

SIR JOSEPH WITTOLL

Ah! oh Lord, my heart aches. Ah! Setter, a rogue of all sides.

SHARPER

Sir Joseph, you had better have pre-engaged this gentleman's pardon: for though Vainlove be so generous to forgive the loss of his mistress, I know not how Heartwell may take the loss of his wife.

[**SYLVIA** unmasks.]

HEARTWELL

My wife! By this light 'tis she, the very cockatrice. O Sharper! Let me embrace thee. But art thou sure she is really married to him?

SETTER

Really and lawfully married, I am witness.

SHARPER

Bellmour will unriddle to you.

[**HEARTWELL** goes to **BELLMOUR**.]

SIR JOSEPH WITTOLL

Pray, madam, who are you? For I find you and I are like to be better acquainted.

SYLVIA

The worst of me is, that I am your wife—

SHARPER

Come, Sir Joseph, your fortune is not so bad as you fear. A fine lady, and a lady of very good quality.

SIR JOSEPH WITTOLL

Thanks to my knighthood, she's a lady—

VAINLOVE

That deserves a fool with a better title. Pray use her as my relation, or you shall hear on't.

CAPTAIN BLUFFE

What, are you a woman of quality too, spouse?

SETTER

And my relation; pray let her be respected accordingly. Well, honest Lucy, fare thee well. I think, you and I have been play-fellows off and on, any time this seven years.

LUCY

Hold your prating. I'm thinking what vocation I shall follow while my spouse is planting laurels in the wars.

CAPTAIN BLUFFE

No more wars, spouse, no more wars. While I plant laurels for my head abroad, I may find the branches sprout at home.

HEARTWELL

Bellmour, I approve thy mirth, and thank thee. And I cannot in gratitude, for I see which way thou art going, see thee fall into the same snare out of which thou hast delivered me.

BELLMOUR

I thank thee, George, for thy good intention; but there is a fatality in marriage, for I find I'm resolute.

HEARTWELL

Then good counsel will be thrown away upon you. For my part, I have once escaped; and when I wed again, may she be—ugly, as an old bawd.

VAINLOVE

Ill-natured, as an old maid—

BELLMOUR

Wanton, as a young widow—

SHARPER
And jealous, as a barren wife.

HEARTWELL
Agreed.

BELLMOUR
Well; 'midst of these dreadful denunciations, and notwithstanding the warning and example before me, I commit myself to lasting durance.

BELINDA
Prisoner, make much of your fetters.

[Giving her hand.]

BELLMOUR
Frank, will you keep us in countenance?

VAINLOVE
May I presume to hope so great a blessing?

ARAMINTA
We had better take the advantage of a little of our friend's experience first.

BELLMOUR
O' my conscience she dares not consent, for fear he should recant. [Aside.] Well, we shall have your company to church in the morning. May be it may get you an appetite to see us fall to before you. Setter, did not you tell me?—

SETTER
They're at the door: I'll call 'em in.

A DANCE

BELLMOUR
Now set we forward on a journey for life. Come take your fellow-travellers. Old George, I'm sorry to see thee still plod on alone.

HEARTWELL
With gaudy plumes and jingling bells made proud, The youthful beast sets forth, and neighs aloud. A morning-sun his tinselled harness gilds, And the first stage a down-hill greensward yields. But, oh— What rugged ways attend the noon of life! Our sun declines, and with what anxious strife, What pain we tug that galling load, a wife. All coursers the first heat with vigour run; But 'tis with whip and spur the race is won.

[Exeunt **OMNES**.]

Spoken by MRS. BARRY.

As a rash girl, who will all hazards run,
And be enjoyed, though sure to be undone,
Soon as her curiosity is over,
Would give the world she could her toy recover,
So fares it with our poet; and I'm sent
To tell you he already does repent:
Would you were all as forward to keep Lent.
Now the deed's done, the giddy thing has leisure
To think o' th' sting, that's in the tail of pleasure.
Methinks I hear him in consideration:
What will the world say? Where's my reputation?
Now that's at stake. No, fool, 'tis out o' fashion.
If loss of that should follow want of wit,
How many undone men were in the pit!
Why that's some comfort to an author's fears,
If he's an ass, he will be tryed by's peers.
But hold, I am exceeding my commission:
My business here was humbly to petition;
But we're so used to rail on these occasions,
I could not help one trial of your patience:
For 'tis our way, you know, for fear o' th' worst,
To be beforehand still, and cry Fool first.
How say you, sparks?
How do you stand affected? I swear, young
Bays within is so dejected,
'Twould grieve your hearts to see him; shall I call him?
But then you cruel critics would so maul him!
Yet may be you'll encourage a beginner;
But how? Just as the devil does a sinner.
Women and wits are used e'en much at one,
You gain your end, and damn 'em when you've done.

William Congreve – A Short Biography

William Congreve was born on January 24th, 1670 in Bardsey in West Yorkshire, to parents William Congreve (1637–1708) and Mary (née Browning; 1636–1715).

When he was two the family moved to London and, at age four, they moved again, this time to the Irish port town of Youghal where his father, a former Cavalier, now served as a lieutenant in the British army.

Congreve's childhood in Ireland included an education at Kilkenny College, where he met Jonathan Swift, who would become a life-long friend, and then university at Trinity College, Dublin.

After graduating he moved to London to study law at Middle Temple. However his interest in studying law soon lessened as the attraction of literature, drama, and the fashionable life began to exert their powerful pull.

Congreve now assumed the pseudonym Cleophil and published a novel he had written at 17 (although accounts vary as to the exact date) called Incognita: or, Love and Duty reconcil'd in 1692.

The work was judged a success and he was welcomed into the London literary world. Congreve quickly became a disciple of the great John Dryden, whom he had met at gatherings of artists and writers at Will's Coffeehouse in Covent Garden in London.

Dryden was a man of immense importance in Literary London and his support would be of great help. This support would also extend to writing several panegyrical introductions for Congreve's later works.

Congreve himself is seen as the playwright who shaped and developed the English comedy of manners through his use of satire and precisely written dialogue.

His first play was performed in 1693 and was an immediate hit. It is interesting to see here how his writing benefited with the roles of women actually now being performed by women. Previously men had performed all the roles but Congreve was quick to take advantage of this change and provide both better nuanced roles and to push the boundaries of what was allowable even further. An actress by the name of Mrs Anne Bracegirdle would be the lead actress in most of his plays.

His first play, The Old Bachelor, was written, he said, to amuse himself during convalescence, and was produced at the Drury Lane Theatre in 1693 and later by the Theatre Royale. It was an enormous success and ran for an entire two-week period when it first opened. To our modern minds this may seem ridiculously short but that was then the way. There were far fewer theatres then and this, coupled with the competition among a large group of playwrights to be performed and an audience who demanded an ever changing schedule of productions meant that whatever the depth of success runs were short, though revivals were plentiful. Congreve was hailed by John Dryden as having written a brilliant first work.

His second play, The Double-Dealer, unfortunately failed to scale the heights of his first. However Congreve continued to write and although his canon is small by the age of 30 he had established the comedy of manners as a genre.

Love for Love, his third play, premiered on April 30th, 1695 at Lincoln's Inn Field and was another major success. This was followed by The Mourning Bride in 1697 and, at the time was very popular, although today is not seen as being of the same standard as his other works.

After the production of Love for Love, Congreve went into theatre management, initially at Lincoln's Inn Fields in 1695. It was also during this period that he wrote some verse although this was merely a sideline to his playwriting abilities.

His final play, The Way of the World debuted in March 1700 and, initially, was considered a complete failure. However over time it has come to be regarded for what it truly is: a masterpiece and is now frequently revived.

As a result of his success and literary merit, he was awarded one of the five positions of commissioner for licensing hackney coaches.

Although his playwrighting career was successful it was also very brief. Five plays authored from 1693 to 1700 would prove the entirety of his output. The audience for these comedy of manners now turned away from these risqué, sexual plays to those with a more stringent moral code. His output from 1700 was restricted to the occasional poem and some translation (notably Molière's Monsieur de Pourceaugnac).

Congreve was particularly upset be a piece written be Jeremy Collier (A Short View of the Immorality and Profaneness of the English Stage), and wrote a rebuttal; "Amendments of Mr. Collier's False and Imperfect Citations."

Alas no further plays were to flow from his pen but Congreve did write librettos for two operas and to begin translating the works of Molière.

His interests now took in politics. Being a member of the influential Whig Kit-Kat Club, helped him obtain various minor political posts, including being named Secretary of the Island of Jamaica by George I in 1714, in spite of being a Whig among Tories.

Regardless of this career change Congreve continued his writing, although it was in a very different style. his works now took the form of poetry as well as many more translations. This time the works of Homer, Juvenal, Ovid, and Horace.

As with so many people of the day, health was an issue. As early as 1710, he suffered both from gout and from cataracts.

The royalties from revivals, as well as a private income, enabled Congreve to live the rest of his life as he wished.

Although Congreve never married and remained single he formed many attachments with prominent actresses and noblewomen for whom he wrote major parts in all his plays. These women included Anne Bracegirdle and Henrietta Godolphin, 2nd Duchess of Marlborough, daughter of the famous general, John Churchill, 1st Duke of Marlborough.

The gossip of the day was that Congreve was father to Henrietta's child, Mary, born in 1723.

Congreve suffered a carriage accident in late September 1728, from which he never recovered and it is thought that he received some sort of debilitating internal injury.

William Congreve died in London on January 19th, 1729, and was buried in Poets' Corner in Westminster Abbey. His will revealed that his entire fortune was left to Henrietta, the Duchess of Marlborough.

William Congreve – A Concise Bibliography

Incognita (Novel) (1692)
The Old Bachelor (1693)
The Double Dealer (1694)
Love for Love (1695)
The Mourning Bride (1697)
The Way of the World (1700)